Civilians and Soldiers

ACHIEVING BETTER COORDINATION

Bruce R. Pirnie

Prepared for the Smith Richardson Foundation

National Security Research Division

RAND

Approved for public release; distribution unlimited

The purpose of this project, sponsored by the Smith Richardson Foundation, Incorporated, is to examine recent experience in complex contingency operations and develop recommendations that would achieve better coordination among civilians and soldiers. H. Smith Richardson and his wife Grace Jones Richardson established the foundation in 1935. Its mission is to help inform important public policy debates through support of pragmatic, policy-relevant research, analysis, and writing. Grants are channeled through three programs: International Security and Foreign Policy, Children and Families at Risk, and Governance.

Coordination is required both within the U.S. government through the interagency process and among actors in the field, including international organizations, regional alliances, and nongovernmental organizations. Of these, the interagency process has caused the greater difficulties and most needs reform. The United States cannot expect to exert leadership if it has not first thought through its own strategy. This report focuses on the interagency process.

During the research phase of this project, we assembled materials on complex contingency operations, interviewed mid- and high-level participants, participated in the Chairman of the Joint Chiefs of Staff's 1998 Peace Operations Seminar, and established a close working relationship with the Directorate for Global Issues and Multilateral Affairs in the National Security Council. During this process, we prepared a brief overview of major players in these operations, including agencies of the U.S. government, agencies within the United Nations system, international and regional agencies, and ad hoc organizations. On the basis of this research, we concluded that the fundamental impediment to better coordination is internal, namely recurrent failures within the U.S. government to develop and pursue coherent policies and strategies.

During the analytic phase of the project, we developed and evaluated alternative models for the interagency process in complex contingency operations, examined the feasibility and utility of advance planning, developed the outline of a generic political-military plan from official and unofficial sources, discerned lessons from the three most significant operations in recent years (Somalia, Haiti, Bosnia), and finally developed recommendations to achieve better coordination, focusing on the internal dynamics of the United States as lead country.

This research was performed within the International Security and Defense Policy Center of RAND. The prospective audience for this research includes decisionmakers and their staffs within the Executive Branch of the U.S. government who are concerned with planning and conduct of complex contingency operations.

Comments and inquiries are welcome and should be addressed to the author Bruce Pirnie.

CONTENTS

Preface iii

Figures ix

Tables xi

Summary xiii

Acknowledgments xix

Abbreviations xxi

Chapter One
   APPROACH 1
   Background 1
   Purpose of the Project 3
   Assumptions 3
   Approach 4
      Phases of the Project 4
      Scope of the Research 4
   Organization Of This Report 6

Chapter Two
   INTRODUCTION 7
   Pattern During the Cold War 7
      Bipartisan Foreign Policy 7
      Two-Sided Struggle 7
      Internationalism in Abeyance 8
      Clear Dichotomies 8
   Changes After the Cold War 9
      Smoldering Debate 9
      Impartiality 9
      Internationalism in Ascent 10
      Blurred Boundaries 10

U.S. Leadership 11
   Critical Need 11
   Uneven Performance 12
Causes of the Uneven Performance 13
   Less-Compelling Rationale 13
   Lack of Confidentiality 14
   Fitful Interagency Coordination 14
   Civilian-Military Divide 15
   Disagreement on the Military's Role 16

Chapter Three
  OVERVIEW OF ORGANIZATIONS 19
  National Security Council 19
  State 20
   Department of State 20
   U.S. Agency for International Development 21
   U.S. Information Agency 21
  Defense 21
   Department of Defense 21
   Military Departments 22
   Joint Chiefs of Staff 22
   Unified Commands 22
  Central Intelligence Agency 23
  Department of Agriculture 23
  Department of Commerce 24
  Department of Energy 24
  Department of Justice 24
  Department of the Treasury 25
  Federal Emergency Management Agency 25
  Overseas Private Investment Corporation 25
  U.S. Congress 26
  United Nations System 26
   United Nations Security Council 27
   United Nations Department of Humanitarian Affairs 27
   Department of Peacekeeping Operations 27
   United Nations Food and Agricultural Organization 28
   United Nations World Food Programme 28
   World Health Organization 28
   United Nations Children's Fund 29
   United Nations High Commissioner for Refugees 29
   United Nations High Commissioner for Human Rights 30
   United Nations Development Programme 30
   United Nations Educational, Scientific and Cultural Organization . . 30

Other International Organizations 30
    International Red Cross and Red Crescent Movement 30
    World Bank 31
    International Monetary Fund 32
Regional Organizations 32
    North Atlantic Treaty Organization 32
    Organization for Security and Cooperation in Europe 33
Ad Hoc Organizations 34
    Contact Group 34
    International Criminal Tribunal for the Former Yugoslavia 34
    Peace Implementation Council 35
    High Representative 35
Nongovernmental Organizations 35
    Catholic Relief Services 36
    Cooperative for Assistance and Relief Everywhere 36
    Medecins Sans Frontieres 36
    Oxfam 36

Chapter Four
ACHIEVING BETTER COORDINATION 39
Attitudes Toward Planning 39
    Interagency Process 40
    Stages of the Process 41
    NSC-Centered Model 41
    Special Representative Model 43
    Combined Model 45
    Evaluating the Models 46
Planning 48
    Need for Advance Planning 48
    Anticipating Crises 52
    Front End of Advance Planning 55
    Political-Military Plans 58
    After-Action Review 58
Field Operations 59
    Lessons from Somalia 60
    Lessons from Haiti 64
    Lessons from Bosnia 69
    Organization of Complex Contingency Operations 78

Chapter Five
RECOMMENDATIONS 83
Achieve Consensus on Complex Contingency Operations 83
Make the Interagency Process Robust 83
Develop and Issue Authoritative Plans 84

Conduct Advance Planning   84
Bring Combatant Commanders into Interagency Planning   84
Invite Non-U.S. Agencies into the Planning Process   84
Encourage Civilian-Military Discourse   85
Improve Interagency Training   85
Establish Interagency Communications to the Field   85
Provide Civilian Surge Capability   85
Exchange Personnel Across Departments   86
Ensure Coordination in the Field   86
Charter Independent After-Action Reviews   86

Appendix
   A. TERMINOLOGY   87
   B. OUTLINE OF A POLITICAL-MILITARY PLAN   89

Bibliography   97

FIGURES

S.1. Model for the Interagency Process xv
4.1. NSC-Centered Model 42
4.2. Special Representative Model 44
4.3. Combined Model 46
4.4. Haiti-Like Scenario 49
4.5. More-Likely Scenario 50
4.6. More-Likely Scenario with Advance Planning 51
4.7. Evaluating Possible Crises Against Criteria 54
4.8. Evaluating Possible Crises Against U.S. Interests 55
4.9. Continue Hope and UNOSOM II 62
4.10. Restore Democracy and UNMIH 67
4.11. Joint Guard and UNMIBH 76
4.12. Organization of a Complex Contingency Operation 80

4.1. Criteria to Evaluate Models 48
4.2. Examples of Potential Crises 52
4.3. Roles Described in the Dayton Agreement 71
A.1. Terms and Definitions 87
B.1. Illustrative Phases of an Operation 92
B.2. Illustrative Event Matrix 93

U.S. LEADERSHIP

U.S. leadership is crucial to the successful conduct of complex contingency operations, but U.S. performance since 1989 has been erratic. Among the causes for this erratic performance are less-compelling rationale, fitful interagency coordination, and disagreement over the military's role.

Less-Compelling Rationale

The rationale for complex contingency operations is prima facie less compelling than the rationale for containing Communism. Why should the United States fight to keep others from fighting? Why should the United States try to reconstitute governments torn apart by their own people? Why should the United States willfully become involved in countries of little geopolitical importance? Unless a more-compelling rationale is offered for complex contingency operations, support for them will remain problematic. The conundrum is how to define U.S. interests in the post–Cold War era. Complex contingency operations are just one aspect, albeit a crucial aspect, of this conundrum.

Fitful Interagency Coordination

Fitful coordination across the departments and agencies of the U.S. government is a major cause of difficulty. If a department is at odds with itself, the departmental head or his deputy can break the impasse. But only the President stands above them all, and he cannot afford to spend time harmonizing their efforts. At the start of the Cold War, Congress addressed this problem in the National Security Act of 1947, establishing the National Security Council (NSC). But over the following half century the NSC has functioned fitfully. Sometimes it works as the law prescribes; sometimes it works in other ways; and sometimes it breaks down.

Disagreement on the Military's Role

There is fundamental disagreement over the use of military forces in complex contingency operations. Generally speaking, the Department of State is more willing to employ force than is the Department of Defense. The usual reluctance of Defense leadership to take on complex contingency operations is understandable. During these contingencies, military forces assume responsibilities that are onerous and easily tend to become indefinite. They are ancillary to the military's primary purpose of fighting the nation's wars, unpopular with Congress, and not well understood by the American public.

The essential problem is not better coordination, but rather a strong national will. Absent a strong national will, the United States is reluctant to risk even minimal casualties and is therefore in constant danger of defeat by very minor opponents who could inflict only a few casualties.

MODEL FOR THE INTERAGENCY PROCESS

An interagency process should not only accommodate, but also promote, strong, continuous leadership, including leadership by men and women who are exclusively concerned with a particular contingency. Without such leadership, an interagency process may drift or cause endless bickering in Washington. Leadership is also important abroad. To make its full influence felt, the United States must be able to confront foreign officials, especially former belligerents, with a person who speaks for the United States and who cannot be circumvented or undermined. (See Figure S.1.)

RECOMMENDATIONS

Achieve Consensus on Complex Contingency Operations

The United States urgently needs national consensus, embracing Congress, opinion-makers, and the public, about the nature and scope of its role in complex contingency operations. Are they a deliberate part of U.S. foreign policy or hesitant improvisations when policy has failed? If the administration cannot obtain broad consensus, it must at least attain consensus in particular cases. Otherwise, support will remain fragile and even slight reverses may cause failure.

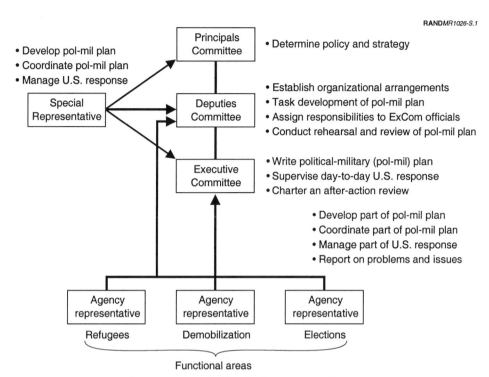

Figure S.1—Model for the Interagency Process

Make the Interagency Process Robust

The interagency process needs better definition to make it robust and productive. It should follow well-understood, firmly established procedures, not be continually reinvented in unpredictable ways. It should demand departmental advice at each level and interdepartmental decisions that are unambiguously expressed and binding on all agencies of the Executive Branch. An optimal model would combine a Special Representative to provide leadership with a tiered system of interagency meetings to develop policy and to make day-by-day decisions.

Develop and Issue Authoritative Plans

Conduct of complex contingency operations needs formal planning to ensure that objectives are clearly understood, that actions are properly sequenced and coordinated, and that appropriate officials are held responsible for attaining objectives. As military commanders issue military plans that are binding on their subordinates, so the President should issue political-military plans that are binding on officers and officials throughout the Executive Branch. The

National Security Advisor would be a natural choice for authentication of political-military plans developed through the interagency process and approved by the President.

Conduct Advance Planning

Presidential Decision Directive–56 (PDD-56) does not specify whether planning should begin in advance of or during crisis. But if planning starts during crisis, there may be insufficient time to prepare plans, coordinate the plans, and rehearse them. Therefore, the United States should plan in advance for those contingencies likely to prompt intervention. Although onset is unpredictable, it is easy to discern where complex contingencies are likely to occur despite U.S. action to prevent and mitigate them. Even if future contingencies occurred in unexpected places, the discipline and experience of advance planning would be transferable to these unexpected contingencies.

Bring Combatant Commanders into Interagency Planning

Currently, regional combatant commanders may not be directly involved in the interagency planning process or they may participate episodically. However, these commanders have a fundamental responsibility to execute military aspects of the complex contingency operations. Moreover, they have extensive experience in their regions and routinely plan for a range of military operations, including many of the aspects associated with complex contingency operations. Working through the Joint Staff, combatant commanders and their representatives should participate directly in interagency planning.

Invite Non-U.S. Agencies into the Planning Process

Non-U.S. agencies, including agencies within the United Nations system and nongovernmental organizations (NGOs), are usually willing to participate in a U.S.-led planning process, although they are not bound by a U.S.-generated plan. For example, relief agencies are usually anxious to learn what protection will be provided and what logistic support they can anticipate receiving through U.S. channels. At the latest, relief agencies should participate during review of a political-military plan. Of course, some parts of U.S. military planning are necessarily classified, but these parts usually do not concern non-U.S. agencies.

Encourage Civilian-Military Discourse

The United States needs discourse on the level of policy and strategy to achieve clarity and to bridge the civilian-military gap. Civilians should articulate goals and ask, not tell, military officers how military force can contribute to attaining them. Military officers should disabuse themselves of the notion that they need only respond to political direction: Civilians badly need military advice to help develop sensible strategy.

Improve Interagency Training

The interagency training prescribed by PDD-56 is not funded and remains inadequately attended. It compares poorly to the more extensive training, exercises, and education conducted by military organizations. This interagency training should be appropriately funded, and participation should be mandatory or strongly encouraged. For greater realism, this training should be conducted together with a military exercise conducted by a regional combatant commander, either on-site or remotely.

Establish Interagency Communications to the Field

In current practice, each department or agency of the Executive Branch has its own channel of communications to the field and no interagency channel, except for communications from the President or a Special Representative speaking for him, exists. As a result, confusion may ensue when various agencies communicate their varying interpretations of what transpired in interagency meetings. To preclude such confusion, there should be a regular channel of communications conveying decisions and instructions from interagency meetings to organizations in the field.

Provide Civilian Surge Capability

During complex contingency operations, a concerned agency often forms a task force to monitor the course of events, marshal its resources, and represent it in the interagency process. Among the agencies of the Executive Branch, only the Department of Defense has adequate surge capability to generate such elements. Other agencies lack such surge capability and therefore might not provide enough experienced personnel and adequate administrative support. There should be provision for surge capability within all agencies that expect to play important roles in complex contingency operations.

Exchange Personnel Across Departments

Under current practice, the task forces or similar entities with day-to-day responsibility for complex contingency operations may or may not include officers or officials from other agencies. It would improve communications and perhaps establish a higher level of mutual confidence if agencies routinely loaned each other personnel. Moreover, such personnel would enrich the process by adding outside expertise. As an example, State and Defense should exchange personnel working on such task forces. In the post–Cold War era, it may also be advisable to develop a broader program of exchange across military and civilian agencies.

Ensure Coordination in the Field

Coordination in the field demands that civilian heads of mission and military force commanders share strategic vision, meaning common understanding of their missions and the implied goals. In addition, they need formal arrangements to facilitate coordination, including combined operations centers, task forces, and exchange of liaison officers. These arrangements should be made in advance because the initial phase of an operation can be crucial.

Charter Independent After-Action Reviews

PDD-56 directs the Executive Committee to charter after-action reviews involving participants and experts. Participants should not direct or appear to direct this process. The temptation to spare people's feelings is far greater on the civilian side, which has no comparable tradition of after-action reports. To ensure impartiality and candor, the Deputies Committee should charter consortiums of well-regarded analytic agencies to conduct reviews. These reviews will inevitably be classified, but an unclassified version should be made widely available to share and profit from the lessons learned.

The author gratefully acknowledges assistance from persons who consented to be interviewed. They spoke with admirable directness and candor, although most officials currently in office understandably requested that their remarks not be attributed to them. In alphabetical order, the author extends thanks to Thomas Adams, Eastern European Assistance Office, Bureau of European and Canadian Affairs, Department of State; Lt. Col. Michael F. Bailey, USA, Military Advisor, Office of Peacekeeping and Humanitarian Operations, Bureau of International Organization Affairs, Department of State; Maj. Mark A. Baker, USAF, Action Officer, Peacekeeping Branch, Global Division, Directorate for Strategic Plans and Policy (J-5); Betram D. Braun, Regional Affairs Officer (Bosnia Desk), Office of South Central European Affairs, Department of State; Brig. Gen. George W. Casey, Jr., USA, Deputy Director of Politico-Military Affairs, Directorate for Strategic Plans and Policy (J-5); Ivo H. Daalder, then Associate Professor, School of Public Affairs, University of Maryland, and former staff member of the National Security Council; Col. Michael J. Dziedzic, USAF, Senior Military Fellow, Institute for National Strategic Studies, National Defense University; Michele Flournoy, Principal Deputy Assistant Secretary of Defense (Strategy); Ambassador Robert Louis Gallucci, Dean of the School of Foreign Service, Georgetown University, and former Ambassador at Large, Department of State; Robert B. Gifford, Office of Policy Planning and Coordination, International Narcotics and Law and Anti-Crime Enforcement Affairs, Department of State; Lt. Col. Michael J. Harwood, USA, Director, Joint Operations and Training, U.S. Army Peacekeeping Institute; Leonard R. Hawley, Global Issues and Multilateral Affairs Directorate, National Security Council; Fred Hill, Director of Special Programs, Foreign Service Institute; Gen. George A. Joulwan, USA (Ret.), former Supreme Allied Commander Europe; Col. Gregory Kaufman, USA, Bosnia Task Force, Office of the Under Secretary of Defense for Policy; L. Erick Kjonnerod, Chief, Security Strategy and Policy Branch, War Gaming and Simulation Center, National Defense University; James ("Jock") Kovey, European Affairs Directorate, National Security Council; Thomas M. Leary, Country Affairs Desk Officer, Office of Central European and

Newly Independent States, U.S. Information Agency; Ellen Leddy, Officer in Charge (Bosnia), Agency for International Development; Col. Douglas E. Lute, USA, Commander, 2nd Armored Cavalry Regiment, and formerly staff officer, Joint Staff (J-5); Paul Marin, Eastern European Desk, Department of Commerce; Mark Medish, Deputy Assistant Secretary of the Treasury, Eurasia and the Middle East; Michael A. Monderer, Director of the Bosnia Task Force, Department of the Treasury; Ambassador Robert Oakley, National Defense University, former Ambassador and Special Envoy to Somalia; Robert M. Perito, Deputy Director, International Criminal Investigative Training Assistance Program, Department of Justice; Julie Schechter, Bosnia Desk Officer, Bureau for Population, Refugees, and Migration, Department of State; Robert M. Scher, Senior Assistant for Strategy Development, Office of the Deputy Assistant Secretary of Defense (Strategy); Douglas R. Smith, Bosnia Task Force, Department of State; Janice M. Stromsen, Director, International Criminal Investigative Training Assistance Program, Department of Justice.

The author expresses appreciation to Nadia Schadlow, International Security and Foreign Policy Program, Smith Richardson Foundation, for her guidance in submitting a research proposal and her subsequent attention to this project. He offers special thanks to Len Hawley, assigned in the Directorate of Global Issues and Multilateral Affairs, National Security Council, for acting as if he were a client during this project: providing materials, helping open doors, and discussing issues as they arose. He expresses appreciation to Ivo Daalder, formerly at the National Security Council and currently at the Brookings Institution, for accomplishing an expert and extremely helpful review of the manuscript in draft. He thanks Sheila Hein, Electronic Media Imaging Center, Pentagon, for help in acquiring the image used on the cover.

The author thanks RAND colleagues: Jennifer Casey for her excellent assistance in the research; Lynn Davis and David Gompert for reflecting on the interagency process from personal experience; Stephen Hosmer for sharing his work on U.S. interests (see Chapter Four); Jerry McGinn for sharing his insights during the project and formally reviewing the draft; Roger Molander for reflecting on the interagency process from personal experience; Luetta Pope for secretarial support; Marten van Heuven for sharing his extensive experience in government and international organizations; Daniel Sheehan for his editing of the draft report; and John White for sharing his recent experience as Deputy Secretary of Defense. The author bears sole responsibility for all errors of fact or judgment in this report.

ASF	Auxiliary Security Force (Somalia)
BATF	Bureau of Alcohol, Tobacco, and Firearms (within Treasury)
CARE	Cooperative for Assistance and Relief Everywhere
CIA	Central Intelligence Agency
CIVPOL	(United Nations) Civilian Police
CJCS	Chairman, Joint Chiefs of Staff
CMOC	Civil-Military Operations Center
CRS	Catholic Relief Services
DART	Disaster Assistance Response Team (within OFDA)
DCI	Director of Central Intelligence
DIA	Defense Intelligence Agency
DOC	Department of Commerce
DoD	Department of Defense
DOE	Department of Energy
DOJ	Department of Justice
DOS	Department of State
DoT	Department of Transportation
DPG	Defense Planning Guidance
DPKO	(United Nations) Department of Peacekeeping Operations
EBRD	European Bank for Reconstruction and Development
EU	European Union
FAO	(United Nations) Food and Agricultural Organization
FEMA	Federal Emergency Management Agency
FSI	Foreign Service Institute (within DOS)
HOC	Humanitarian Operations Center
IBRD	International Bank for Reconstruction and Development (within the World Bank)
ICITAP	International Criminal Investigative Training Assistance Program (within DOJ)
ICRC	International Committee of the Red Cross
ICTY	International Criminal Tribunal for the Former Yugoslavia
IDA	International Development Association (within the World Bank)

IFOR	Implementation Force
IMF	International Monetary Fund
INS	Immigration and Naturalization Service (within DOJ)
IPTF	International Police Task Force
JCS	Joint Chiefs of Staff
JSCP	Joint Strategic Capabilities Plan
MEF	Marine Expeditionary Force
MICIVIH	International Civilian Mission in Haiti
MNF	Multinational Force
MSF	*Medecins Sans Frontieres* (Doctors Without Borders)
MSU	Multinational Security Unit (in Bosnia)
NAC	North Atlantic Council
NATO	North Atlantic Treaty Organization
NCA	National Command Authority
NIST	National Intelligence Support Teams
NMS	National Military Strategy
NGO	Nongovernmental organization
NSA	National Security Agency
NSC	National Security Council
OFDA	Office of Foreign Disaster Relief (within USAID)
OHR	Office of the High Representative
OPIC	Overseas Private Investment Corporation
OSCE	Organization for Security and Cooperation in Europe
PDD	Presidential Decision Directive
PIC	Peace Implementation Council
PRD	Presidential Review Directive
SACEUR	Supreme Allied Commander Europe
SACLANT	Supreme Allied Commander Atlantic
SF	(U.S. Army) Special Forces
SFOR	Stabilization Force (Bosnia)
SRSG	Special Representative of the Secretary General
UCP	Unified Command Plan
UNDHA	United Nations Department of Humanitarian Affairs
UNDP	United Nations Development Programme
UNESCO	United Nations Educational, Scientific and Cultural Organization
UNHCHR	United Nations High Commissioner for Human Rights
UNHCR	United Nations High Commissioner for Refugees
UNICEF	United Nations Children's Fund
UNITAF	Unified Task Force (Somalia)
UNMIBH	United Nations Mission in Bosnia and Herzegovina
UNMIH	United Nations Mission in Haiti
UNOSOM I	First United Nations Operation in Somalia

UNOSOM II	Second United Nations Operation in Somalia
UNPREDEP	United Nations Preventive Deployment Force (Macedonia)
UNPROFOR	United Nations Protection Force
UNSC	United Nations Security Council
UNSMIH	United Nations Support Mission in Haiti
UNTMIH	United Nations Transition Mission in Haiti
UNTSO	United Nations Truce Supervision Organization
USACOM	U.S. Atlantic Command
USAID	U.S. Agency for International Development
USDA	U.S. Department of Agriculture
USIA	U.S. Information Agency
WEU	Western European Union
WFP	World Food Programme
WHO	World Health Organization
WMD	Weapons of mass destruction

Chapter One

APPROACH

This chapter outlines background, purpose of the project, assumptions, approach, and organization of the report.

BACKGROUND

During the Cold War, the United States worked through the U.N. Security Council to attain important goals of American foreign policy. A series of peace operations in the Near East helped reduce the risk of Israeli-Arab wars that might compel the United States to abandon its role as mediator, which might have increased Soviet influence with the Arab states. The Congo operation (1960–1964) forestalled Soviet intervention on behalf of Marxist elements. The Cyprus operation (1964–present) helped avert a war between Greece and Turkey and prevent Soviet support for a friendly regime on Cyprus. But during the Cold War, U.S.-Soviet rivalries continually caused impasses in the Security Council.

After European Communism collapsed in 1989, the United States saw opportunities to make much greater use of the Security Council. It sponsored and encouraged a wide range of more ambitious peace operations, including several that it led and dominated. An operation in Cambodia (1992–1993) helped implement the Geneva Accords that ended Vietnamese occupation. An operation in El Salvador (1992–1995) helped reconcile the factions and initiate democratic reform after a protracted civil war in which the United States had been heavily interested. The United States led an intervention in Somalia (December 1992–May 1993) that became a humiliating debacle after the United States withdrew most of its forces. After long hesitation, it led an operation in Haiti (September 1994–March 1995) that restored the legitimate government and ended attempts at massive illegal migration to the United States. After first attempting to stay clear of the Balkan wars, it led an operation in Bosnia (December 1995–present) that freed its allies from a major embarrassment, restored the prestige of the North Atlantic Treaty Organization (NATO), and reasserted U.S. leadership in Europe.

U.S. leadership is vital in more ambitious peace operations. Without this leadership, such operations are likely to fail if they are attempted at all. The countries participating in Second United Nations Operation in Somalia (UNOSOM II) not only failed to implement the Addis Ababa Agreements, but could not even deploy their forces safely without U.S. help. The countries participating in United Nations Protection Force (UNPROFOR) in former Yugoslavia, including three permanent members of the Security Council, failed miserably when the United States refused to lead. Humiliating failures of the United Nations Protection Force contrast starkly with the undeniable successes of the U.S.-led Implementation Force.

Military success, however brilliant, does not suffice. It would be shortsighted and self-defeating to concentrate excessively on the military part of peace operations because military objectives are more easily attained. In some cases, military operations are chiefly important because they establish preconditions for civilian activities that are critical to an enduring peace. Civilian activities play a vital role, especially with regard to human rights, humanitarian aid, electoral activities, normalization of life, and reconstruction. No outside power, not even the United States leading a strong international coalition, can ensure viable government, much less reconstruct society without enthusiastic cooperation of the peoples involved. Working through the U.N. system, the United States can facilitate fundamental reform if the peoples involved want it and will work to achieve it.

Since the end of the Cold War, the United States has undertaken more and more ambitious peace operations. These are intended not merely to stop hostilities, but also to create the preconditions of enduring peace through respect for human rights, democratic practice, new governmental structures, and regeneration of economic life. Success in these complex operations demands close coordination of military and civilian efforts, but the United States has difficulty achieving this coordination even among its own agencies, to say nothing of the various international, national, and nongovernmental organizations (NGOs) usually involved.

To be an effective leader, the United States must develop strategies that envision how civilian and military efforts will complement each other to promote enduring peace. It must establish relationships and procedures to ensure that these efforts are well coordinated even in the face of rapidly changing situations. If the United States fails to coordinate civilian and military efforts, it will experience failures that discredit more ambitious peace operations and erode both domestic support and respect for U.S. leadership abroad.

PURPOSE OF THE PROJECT

The purpose of this project is to examine recent experience in complex contingency operations that have civilian and military aspects and to develop recommendations that would achieve better coordination among civilians and soldiers.

This study should help senior policymakers make informed judgments on two levels: broad policy to improve coordination of peace operations and specific choices during actual operations. On the broad policy level, it offers recommendations to gain systemic improvement in the way that civilian and military efforts are coordinated.

ASSUMPTIONS

At the outset of this project, we made the following basic assumptions:

- Bad governance and national, ethnic, and religious antagonisms will continue to cause conflicts.

- Leading states will intervene in some of these conflicts, both for moral reasons and out of self-interest.

- International organizations will remain too weak and inefficient to control such interventions until conditions become stable.

- The United States will be an indispensable leader, both for its moral stature and its global power.

We did *not* assume that such interventions, currently termed "complex contingency operations," should have ambitious goals and long duration. To take a current example, we did not assume that the United States should attempt to reconstitute a unified government in Bosnia and Herzegovina that includes Croats, Muslims, and Serbs and to this end should conduct operations in Bosnia indefinitely. Perhaps the United States should just enforce the military provisions of Dayton and let the parties decide whether they want a unified government, knowing that they would almost certainly partition the country. Even in this latter case, the operation would include civilian and military components and their close coordination would be important to success.

APPROACH

Phases of the Project

Throughout the project, we used a historical-analytic method that abstracts from specific events to generate ideal types. We conducted the project in three phases.

During the first phase of the project, we assembled materials relevant to co-ordination of civilian and military aspects of operations in Bosnia, Haiti, and Somalia. Simultaneously, we conducted interviews with mid- and high-level participants whose expert knowledge enriched the official record.

During the second phase, we traced interactions among civilian and military organizations in the context of unfolding operations. We assessed the quality of these interactions and their effects on the conduct of operations. From these historically specific examples, but without being bound by them, we developed paradigms, particularly for the interagency process.

During the third phase of the project, we evaluated the intrinsic usefulness of these paradigms by applying a set of criteria. Finally, we developed recommendations to improve long-term coordination.

Scope of the Research

We assembled materials using on-line databases, published documents, files maintained by government offices and analytic agencies, and interviews with mid- and high-level participants who can significantly expand understanding of other sources. These materials included resolutions of the Security Council and reports by the Secretary General, departments, and specialized agencies within the U.N. system. They also included reports by regional security organizations, public statements from NGOs, periodical literature, monographs, and books. At the same time, we developed a unique source of information through interviews with participants that focused on the problems of coordination.

We examined operations in Somalia, Haiti, and Bosnia—the three major complex contingency operations led by the United States in the post–Cold War period. Contingencies on this scale are exceptional, and they generate exceptional effort within an administration.

Bosnia is exceptional because it provokes long-term media attention, provokes scrutiny from Congress, demands extraordinary commitment of resources, and may affect the popularity and prestige of an administration. Such contingencies as Angola, El Salvador, and Rwanda do not have such characteristics and therefore do not require the same sustained attention. The important difference lies, of course, in an administration's decision to lead and participate in a major international effort. The latter three contingencies were not intrinsically less important—Rwanda was the most grotesque and heart-wrenching violation of human rights since Cambodia—but they were less important to the United States because it chose not to become directly involved on a large scale.

We made extensive use of interviews, as reflected in the acknowledgments. To elicit candor, these interviews were not for attribution unless the subject wished it, almost never the case for a person in official position. These interviews were time-consuming, requiring one to three hours to conduct, several hours to transcribe into a usable format, and still more time to correlate, but the results were invaluable. Decisionmaking and implementation are idiosyncratic and heavily influenced by departmental politics and personal relationships. To understand such factors, interviews are indispensable. Organizational charts, Presidential Decision Directives, joint publications, field manuals, and other official documents are not necessarily inaccurate, but they can mislead. They tend to present an idealized facade that conceals the lessons of the past. To a commendable extent, military after-action reports are an exception; they depict problems frankly and recommend solutions.

We have not captured the rich color and drama of recent history, but we have seen enough to realize that complex contingency operations are all-too-human undertakings heavily affected by exigencies of the moment and forceful personalities. For the specialist in such operations, it is sobering to realize that they are usually peripheral to an administration, attracting far less concerted attention than domestic affairs. Precisely for this reason, such operations can have an entrepreneurial air, affording greater opportunities for endeavor and even heroism.

Development and implementation of Presidential Decision Directive–56 (PDD-56) was a focus for much of this research. PDD-56 aims to promote better coordination through an interagency process focused on a political-military plan embracing civilian and military agencies. It does not explicitly address advance planning, and it assumes a model for the interagency process that may be less than optimal. It concerns coordination within the U.S. government and says little about how coordination should be effected outside Washington. But the ideas contained in PDD-56 are important and persuasive to many people, especially to younger military officers who accept the necessity for complex contingency operations, are painfully aware of current shortfalls, and yearn to see such operations conducted with the efficiency characteristic of military operations. Such a standard is probably unattainable, but implementation of PDD-56, incomplete as it is, would effect great improvement.

ORGANIZATION OF THIS REPORT

Chapter Two (Introduction) outlines major developments since 1989, points out the need for U.S. leadership, notes uneven performance, and suggests some causes for this vagary, especially disagreement on the U.S. military's proper role. Chapter Three (Overview of Organizations) sketches the roles of selected organizations in conducting complex contingency operations, including a sample of ad hoc governmental organizations designed to deal with current operations in Bosnia. Chapter Four (Achieving Better Coordination) discusses ways of improving coordination between civilians and soldiers, starting with the interagency process in Washington. It sketches three schemes for the interagency process, evaluates these, and selects the optimal one. It makes a case for advance planning and demonstrates that the United States can anticipate what crises are likely and would involve its interests. It explores the front end of advance planning and after-action review. It then turns to field operations and draws lessons from complex contingency operations conducted in Somalia, Haiti, and Bosnia to date. Chapter Five (Recommendations) makes recommendations based on the foregoing analysis that would improve civilian-military coordination. Appendix A (Terminology) defines key terms used in the report. Appendix B (Outline of a Political-Military Plan) presents the framework of a political-military plan drawn from several sources.

Chapter Two

INTRODUCTION

The end of the Cold War had the paradoxical effect of magnifying U.S. power while removing the chief rationale for its use. U.S. leadership remains indispensable, but the United States seems unsure when to lead and has compiled a mixed record in complex contingency operations. There are multiple causes for this uneven performance, including a divide between the civilian and military sides of U.S. government and disagreement over the military's appropriate role in complex contingency operations.

PATTERN DURING THE COLD WAR

Bipartisan Foreign Policy

During the Cold War, there was broad, bipartisan consensus that the United States had to contain Communist power, especially the Soviet Union and its satellites. Communist power was despotic, militaristic, and brutally oppressive, an enemy that united practically all factions in U.S. politics with the partial exception of the extreme left. Any administration could expect support for foreign policy aimed at containment of Communism. Although strong, this consensus was not unlimited. It showed severe strain during the Korean War and eventually broke down during the Vietnam War. However, polls showed that the American public opposed not war itself but rather unclear purpose and indecisive strategy.

Two-Sided Struggle

Americans tended to perceive the world as divided between two antithetical entities, free countries and the Communist powers. In this two-sided struggle, they expected other states to join one camp or the other and were unsympathetic to the nonaligned movement that sought a middle way. Even peace operations were viewed in this light and had this rationale. The United States supported a protracted and rather embarrassing operation in the Congo primarily to preclude takeover by a faction ideologically aligned with Moscow. It supported an operation in Cyprus partially to contain a Cypriot regime that it saw as dangerously left-leaning.

Internationalism in Abeyance

During this period, internationalism was largely in eclipse. The United States willingly used the United Nations to contain Communist power, most notably during the Korean War fought under a United Nations Command. But the Security Council merely authorized this command and its U.S. commander in chief reported to the U.S. President, not to the Security Council. Such a command became possible only because the Soviet Union had unwisely absented itself from the Security Council. One or another of the permanent members would normally prevent the Security Council from acting in any situation that affected the worldwide struggle between democracy and Communism, which included practically every situation. When the General Assembly became a sounding board for anticolonialism aimed at the United States and its allies, the United States became impatient with and even mildly contemptuous of the United Nations, despite having founded it.

Clear Dichotomies

The most obvious dichotomy was between peace and war. Despite rhetorical reference to a Cold War, the United States did not feel itself to be at war and indeed took great pains to avoid open conflict with its chief adversary, the Soviet Union. The crises over Berlin and Cuba illustrate not so much the antagonism between the sides as their exquisite care to avoid war that neither perceived as being winnable or in its interest. Indeed, the chief reaction to the Cuban crisis was general relief that it was over and determination not to take things so far again. On the two occasions when the United States did go to war, the American public clearly perceived a difference and expected other rules to apply. It abhorred protracted indecision, which seemed normal in peacetime but intolerable in war. It regarded war as abnormal and demanded decisive action to restore the normal condition of peace.

The dichotomy of peace and war implied a clear distinction between the civilian side and the military side of government. The civilian side was normally active because the country was normally at peace. The military side normally trained for war and became active during war. Considering that the primary effects of applying military force are to kill people and to destroy things, such inactivity was rightly regarded as a blessing. The chief value of military forces was not to fight wars but to deter them according to the ancient maxim, "*Si vis pacem para bellum.*"[1]

Still another dichotomy was between administrative activities and operations. The usual activities of government were (and still are) administrative, as reflected by the term "administration" in reference to the Executive Branch. Administrative activities are day-to-day routines that form predictable patterns and have aggregate, not individual characteristics. The civilian side was almost exclusively administrative, and the military side was usually administrative, excluding exercises. By contrast, operations are exceptional actions that break from day-to-day routines. During the Cold War, military operations were relatively infrequent, making the dichotomy sharper.

CHANGES AFTER THE COLD WAR

Smoldering Debate

The bipartisan consensus of the Cold War has given way to a smoldering debate over foreign policy. Almost no one doubts that the United States is an exceptional nation, the world's finest example of democratic practice and respect for human rights, but there is little consensus on the best foreign policy for such a power. Most Americans would reject a crusade for American values as unworldly and true isolationism as unworthy, but if a middle-of-the-road consensus exists, its outlines are still indistinct. Consider, for example, the remarkable lack of enthusiasm for Haiti and Bosnia despite dramatic success, at least of the U.S. military. In Haiti, the United States overthrew a despicable regime that preyed on its own people and gave Haitians their first real chance at democracy, yet the action won little praise. In Bosnia, the United States ended a war that had outraged conscience and opened at least the vista of a secure future for the entire European continent led by a revitalized NATO, yet Congress remains deeply skeptical and the administration hardly dares take credit for its successes.

Impartiality

Arguably, most struggles were always complex beneath an imposed schema of two-sided confrontation between Communist power and democracies. Absent this schema, struggles appeared in their full complexity and moral ambivalence. It was not always clear which side the United States should support, or whether it should support any side at all. An alternative was to adopt the attitude of

---

[1] "If you want peace, prepare for war," Flavius Vegetius Renatus, Epitoma Rei Militaris (a.k.a. De Re Militari), fourth century, A.D.

impartiality traditionally associated with U.N. peace operations. In Somalia and Bosnia, the United States was impartial. It supported Security Council resolutions that did not identify unique aggressors, instead holding all parties responsible. It opposed the Aideed faction in Somalia and the Pale regime in Bosnia (after the Dayton Agreement) not because they were uniquely aggressive but because they had violated their agreements with other parties.

Internationalism in Ascent

The end of the Cold War brought an often-remarked increase in internationalism, more precisely in multilateral operations to restore or preserve peace. When the United States and Russia became friendly powers, the impasse in the Security Council was broken, leading to a flood of resolutions, including many forceful ones that the Security Council subsequently declined to enforce. Peace operations became far more prevalent, and many had a new character. Great powers, formerly precluded on principle, could now take part, opening new vistas of enforcement that would previously have been impractical. Neither the debacle in Somalia nor years of humiliation in Bosnia prevented the United States and its allies from attempting new peace operations, albeit with considerable reluctance and against great skepticism in Congress.

Blurred Boundaries

The more ambitious post–Cold War peace operations, currently styled "complex contingency operations," blur the traditional distinction between peace and war. For example, the United States now has combat troops deployed in Bosnia, patrolling areas of potential strife and constantly prepared to enforce the military provisions of a peace agreement. They could at any moment become involved in combat and are even more likely to become involved in civil disturbances that indigenous police and NATO-controlled gendarmerie cannot master. No one would call this situation war, but is it peace in the usual sense of the word? It would appear that complex contingency operations occur in a twilight zone between the light of peace and the darkness of war.

Just as peace and war have become blurred, so too the distinctions between civilian and military have become less distinct. Despite some understandable reluctance, the military has accepted missions outside of war-fighting. It has supported indigenous police and done police work itself, at least for interim periods. It has provided medical care, restored utilities, repaired infrastructure, and facilitated elections. At the same time, civilians cooperate more closely with military counterparts. For example, officials in many European countries observe with astonishment and some envy that U.S. diplomats habitually travel in the company of high-ranking military officers. Such close and continuous cooperation among civilian and military officials would be unthinkable in their governments where the two sides are kept at arm's length.

Perhaps the most unsettling change for the U.S. government is a blurred distinction between administration and operations. Complex contingency operations demand that civilian agencies of the U.S. government become operational, i.e., take active roles in unique actions outside their day-to-day routines. Such operations make demands both in planning and implementation that not only fall outside their normal routines but also are at odds with their culture. In effect, they are expected to adopt techniques and procedures familiar to military officers but quite foreign to their civilian counterparts.

U.S. LEADERSHIP

U.S. leadership is crucial to the successful conduct of complex contingency operations, but the United States is uncertain about how to conduct them. Its performance since 1989 has been erratic, and little evidence shows it is learning from its experience in any consistent or systematic way.

Critical Need

The ascent of internationalism, especially as manifested in U.N. peace operations, does not imply that U.S. leadership is less needed than during the Cold War. Experience over the past decade has shown that U.S. leadership remains the sine qua non for effective action, whether through international organizations, regional alliances, or less formal coalitions. Americans' sometimes bumptious assertions that their country is superior to all others, the only global power, indeed a "superpower" in a league of its own, thus have a kernel of truth. In really difficult situations and especially when force is required, nothing works well or even works at all without the United States. In an especially succinct formulation:

> If the United States does not lead, no one else will. This is not disguised U.S. exceptionalism, but simply diplomatic and military reality. (Natsios, 1997, p. 161.)

Early in the Clinton administration, Madeleine Albright outlined an approach to world leadership she called "assertive multilateralism":

> Much of our credibility as a superpower—and we must in my view remain one—will depend on our ability to manage our approach to these four groups [established states, emerging democracies, defiant regimes, failed societies]. Though sometimes we will act alone, our foreign policy will necessarily point towards multilateral engagement. But unless the United States also exercises leadership within collective bodies like the U.N., there is a risk that multi-

lateralism will not serve our national interests well. In fact it may undermine our interests.

These two realities, multilateral engagement and U.S. leadership within collective bodies, require an assertive multilateralism which would advance U.S. policy goals. (Albright, 1993.)

U.S. leadership is obviously crucial when military action is required to terminate conflict but is just as crucial during subsequent phases. Introduction of military forces is the most dramatic phase of a complex contingency operation but in most respects is also the simplest and most easily executed. When the United States appears as the leader of an international force to compel compliance with provisions that parties have already ratified, few parties are inclined to have second thoughts. Subsequent phases, which usually require both civilian and military efforts, often in close cooperation, are more complex and difficult to execute. Who but the United States could lead others in both the civilian and military spheres simultaneously? Certainly not the United Nations, which cannot control military forces effectively and has difficulty coordinating even its own departments and agencies. In the words of Robert Gelbard:

An important aspect of our leadership is our ability to integrate the civilian and military aspects of the peace effort. As the history of the negotiations shows, only the United States has the resources, flexibility, and will to pull together all the strands of the complex implementation effort effectively. (Gelbard, 1998.)

Uneven Performance

In three complex contingency operations (Somalia, Haiti, Bosnia), U.S. performance has been uneven and exhibited no consistent tendency. During its first months in Somalia, the United States intimidated the warring factions by an impressive show of force, secured the delivery of humanitarian aid, and made a start toward disarmament. But thereafter it withdrew most of its forces and attempted to lead a weaker U.N. operation with a more ambitious mandate: full implementation of the Addis Ababa Agreements, implying that the so-called "warlords" would have to relinquish their power in a newly constituted state. A humiliating debacle ensued that contributed to the apologetic air of PDD-25, essentially a promise to follow certain rudimentary and long-understood principles of military art, such as articulating a clear mission.

Having learned from Somalia, the United States approached Haiti in a more disciplined way. The United States enjoyed great advantages in Haiti: the opposing military forces were trivial; the legitimate government was extremely popular; the area of operations was only hours distant; and the United States could choose its own time to act. The United States knew that deposing the military regime would be easy, but reconstructing the country would be arduous, so it planned in some detail for this more difficult phase. Although implementation was sometimes ragged, most participants felt that the procedures were appropriate. These were codified several years later in PDD-56.

Two years after intervening in Haiti, the United States entered Bosnia in the largest, most complicated, and arguably most important contingency operation since the end of the Cold War. It should have applied the lessons learned in past operations, but it did not. Instead, the United States organized the Bosnia operation in a fragmented way, reserving military operations for itself and offering civilian affairs to the Europeans with little mechanism for coordination. The interagency process that lies at the heart of PDD-56 broke down, and the United States drifted through the first year and a half of operations with no coherent strategy. This situation improved greatly when a determined Special Representative succeeded in acquiring special authority, but even today it remains unclear whether the United States is fully committed to its ostensible goal—re-creation of a multiethnic or multinational state—and would sustain adversity to accomplish it.

CAUSES OF THE UNEVEN PERFORMANCE

Why is the United States making hard work of these post–Cold War operations? Why is the global power that faced down the Soviet Union having difficulty with lesser opponents? Several causes are apparent.

Less-Compelling Rationale

The rationale for complex contingency operations is prima facie less compelling than the rationale for containing Communism that sustained the United States through the Cold War. It was easy to frame a persuasive case for containing Communism, the menacing antithesis of American values. It is more difficult to persuade Americans that they should undertake and sustain complex contingency operations. Why should the United States fight to keep others from fighting? Why not let them fight until a victor emerges? Why should the United States try to reconstitute governments torn apart by their own people? Will they not tear them apart again for the same reasons? Why should the United States willfully become involved in countries of little geopolitical importance that most Americans could not even find on a map? Unless a persuasive rationale is offered for complex contingency operations, support for them will remain problematic. The conundrum is how to define U.S. interests in the post–Cold War era. Complex contingency operations are just one aspect, albeit a crucial aspect, of this conundrum.

Lack of Confidentiality

To conduct complex operations successfully, the United States needs to foster strategic discourse at high levels of government, but such discourse requires confidentiality. Government officials have a natural reluctance to carry on frank discussions that may become public, but official Washington is so notoriously indiscreet that even principals' meetings may appear in the next day's press. In the words of Richard Holbrooke:

> it was a sad truth of modern Washington that no reporting sent through normal State Department channels—no matter how it was "slugged" for distribution—was safe from the risks of uncontrolled distribution and leaks. (Holbrooke, 1998, p. 135.)

Fitful Interagency Coordination

Fitful coordination across the departments and agencies of the U.S. government is a major cause of difficulty:

> "Okay," the President said. "But I am frustrated that the air campaign is not better coordinated with the diplomatic effort."

> This was an astute observation. The same point troubled me deeply; there was no mechanism or structure within the Administration to coordinate such interagency issues. I wanted to tell the President that this problem required immediate attention. But relations among the NSC, State, and Defense were not something an Assistant Secretary of State could fix. (Holbrooke, 1998, p. 145.)[2]

If a department is at odds with itself, the departmental head or his deputy can break the impasse. But who makes the departments work in harmony? Only the President stands above them all, but he cannot afford to spend time harmonizing their efforts. At the start of the Cold War, Congress addressed this problem in the National Security Act of 1947, establishing the National Security Council (NSC). But over the following half century the NSC has functioned fitfully. Sometimes it works as the law prescribes; sometimes it works in other ways; and sometimes it breaks down.

The NSC can be viewed from two perspectives: as a body composed of statutory members (or their deputies) and as a permanent staff to support the work of the council, headed by the National Security Advisor. The statutory members are at the apex of the Executive Branch, fully empowered to make any decision. But to support their decisionmaking, someone needs to study problems, identify

---

[2]In this case, not only was the interagency process involved, but also a NATO chain of command.

issues, and analyze options. The permanent staff bears primary responsibility for this important work, and it must maintain a delicate balance. If it is too assertive, departmental advice may be stifled, but if it is too diffident the departments may bicker endlessly.

Officials in the Department of Defense (DoD), especially military officers, tend to favor a strong NSC. They expect it to integrate efforts, much as military staffs do, and are frustrated when integration does not occur. Officials in the Department of State tend to oppose a strong NSC because they view it as a rival. But both departments may actually prefer a weak NSC when their desiderata are being met. For example, they may conclude an interdepartmental bargain that contains inconsistencies and prefer not to start an interagency process that would bring these inconsistencies to light.

Civilian-Military Divide

In addition, there is a deep divide, becoming at times a chasm, between the civilian and military sides of the U.S. government. This divide has several aspects.

Tolerance for Ambiguity. Civilian agencies generally and the Department of State in particular have high tolerance for ambiguity. Foreign Service officers assume ambiguity as a normal state of affairs: every issue can be seen from different perspectives; alignments with other countries shift constantly; nothing is ever quite what it seems; and tomorrow may hold surprises. Their most prized skill is negotiation, an activity that offers endless ambiguities, sometimes even in its outcomes. In strong contrast, military officers must reduce ambiguity to a minimum. They assume what they cannot determine and proceed on these assumptions to make definite plans. Their stock-in-trade is action, often of the most direct and brutal nature. Military force ultimately means killing people or threatening to kill them, an activity that should not entail ambiguity.

Attitudes toward Planning. With some exceptions, civilian agencies are skeptical about planning beyond the programmatic level. They tend to regard plans as schedules that are seldom worth the effort because they will be overtaken by events. In the military, plans are indispensable. The military must plan some things (e.g., command relationships, communications nets, latest arrival times, target sets) in elaborate detail to prevent chaos. After years of experience, most military officers have a sophisticated understanding of the planning process. They recognize that no plan is ever executed as written even when unopposed, much less when an opposing force intrudes. They still regard the planning process as indispensable because it produces a shared understanding of the commander's intent and a framework for improvisation.

Disparity in Resources. There is gross disparity between the resources controlled by civilian agencies and those controlled by the military. The
Department of State is notoriously strapped for cash, even to pay for its own
day-to-day activities, much less to address crises. Most civilian agencies, even
those that dispense large sums of money, have limited resources for their own
use. In comparison, the military establishment, even within today's tight budgets, has enormous resources and ability to make things happen. This disparity
is especially great if time is taken into account. The U.S. Agency for International Development (USAID) could allocate funds and design a program to
have some other agency build a bridge in Bosnia next year, but from its own
resources, the Department of Defense could build that bridge next month,
sooner if need be. This disparity causes problems for the Department of
Defense, and it resents being pressured by other agencies of government to
accomplish tasks outside its normal missions merely because it has the
resources.

Disagreement on the Military's Role

There is fundamental disagreement over the use of military forces in complex
contingency operations. Generally speaking, the Department of State is more
willing to employ force and less apprehensive about ancillary missions than is
the Department of Defense. Gen. Colin Powell, USA (Ret.), recounts these disparate attitudes:

> The debate [on Bosnia] exploded at one session when Madeleine Albright, our
> ambassador to the UN, asked me in frustration, "What's the point of having this
> superb military that you're always talking about if we can't use it?" I thought I
> would have an aneurysm. American GIs were not toy soldiers to be moved
> about on some sort of global game board. . . . I told Ambassador Albright that
> the U.S. military would carry out any mission it was handed, but that my advice
> would always be that the tough political goals had to be set first. (Powell with
> Persico 1995, pp. 576–577.)

From Ambassador Albright's perspective, the U.S. military was an underused
instrument of American foreign policy; it should not be held idle, waiting for
wars that might never occur. From General Powell's perspective, the future
Secretary of State was too eager to use force without having thought through
the purpose.

The usual reluctance of Defense Department leadership to take on complex
contingency operations is understandable. During these contingencies, military forces assume responsibilities, often including law enforcement, normally
reserved to sovereign states. Such responsibilities are onerous and easily tend
to become indefinite, as currently evidenced by Bosnia. They are ancillary to
the military's fundamental purpose of fighting the nation's wars, and they

divert scarce resources at a time when the military may already be losing its fine edge. Moreover, they are unpopular with Congress and not well understood by the American public.

U.S. military officers and many civilians believe that support for complex contingency operations is fragile. It could break the moment casualties are incurred, as happened in Somalia. As a result, the U.S. military is obsessed with force protection during these operations, to the point where some other activities are hampered. Ironically, training causes a higher rate of casualties than did operations in Haiti and Bosnia. But training casualties are routine and attract little attention, while casualties during contingency operations are exceptional and attract much attention. The essential problem is uncertain national will. It cannot be solved by the military and requires attention at the highest levels of national leadership. If the United States considers these operations important, it should be willing to risk low casualties. Otherwise, the world's greatest power is in constant danger of defeat by very minor powers, even by criminal bands that can inflict such casualties.

Chapter Three

OVERVIEW OF ORGANIZATIONS

Complex contingency operations feature an enormous cast of highly varied characters, some familiar to the nonspecialist and others more exotic. This section offers a brief overview of the most important actors, including U.S. government agencies, the United Nations system, a few other important international agencies, a sample of regional organizations, and a brief mention of NGOs. There is enormous disparity in the internal resources of these various actors. At one extreme, the U.S. Department of Defense can deploy powerful forces almost anywhere on the globe and support them with a microcosm of America's high standard of living. At another extreme, the United Nations Department of Peacekeeping Operations has very few internal resources and must develop every operation from scratch using oddly assorted national contingents. In the area of humanitarian assistance, most of these organizations primarily manage projects that other organizations (governments, private corporations, and NGOs) accomplish.

NATIONAL SECURITY COUNCIL

The National Security Act of 1947 initially established the NSC as the highest-level body to consider national security issues reflecting practice during World War II. Its statutory members are the President, Vice President, Secretary of State, Secretary of Defense, and secretaries and under secretaries of other executive departments at the pleasure of the President. The Assistant to the President for National Security Affairs, commonly called the National Security Advisor, is not a statutory member of the council. He is appointed by the President to coordinate the council's activities and to oversee its permanent staff. The Chairman of the Joint Chiefs of Staff (CJCS) is the principal military advisor to the NSC. The Director of Central Intelligence (DCI) may attend and participate in meetings of the council. The NSC issues inter alia PDDs that promulgate decisions, set objectives, and codify procedures and Presidential Review Directives (PRDs) that direct policy studies. The NSC has a responsibility to integrate effort of the Executive Branch through the interagency process. (See

Chapter Four.) In addition, it serves as the President's personal staff for security matters. PDD-56 accords the NSC a central role in planning and coordinating civilian and military aspects of complex contingency operations, a role it actually performed to some extent with regard to Haiti.

STATE

Department of State

The Department of State (DOS) has a primary responsibility for formulating and implementing foreign policy. The Secretary of State is the ranking member of the Cabinet and fourth in succession to the Presidency. Assistant secretaries head seven regional bureaus (e.g., Western Hemispheric Affairs) that do not correlate with areas of responsibility under the unified command plan. Within European and Canadian Affairs, the Eastern European Assistance Office currently coordinates economic assistance to various countries in Eastern Europe, including Bosnia. Regional bureaus are subdivided to the level of Desk Officers responsible for single countries or groups of small countries. In addition, the Secretary of State creates ad hoc organizations to deal with particular problems. For example, an Ambassador at Large was named in September 1997 to deal with international war crimes. A small task force within the department currently supports the Special Representative for Bosnia.

Other elements have particular functions. The Assistant Secretary for International Narcotics and Law Enforcement Affairs oversees police affairs abroad, for example the International Police Task Force (IPTF) in Bosnia, and gives direction to the International Criminal Investigative Training Assistance Program (ICITAP) in the Department of Justice. The Bureau of International Organization Affairs oversees most U.N. operations. The Bureau for Population, Refugees, and Migration works with the United Nations High Commissioner for Refugees (UNHCR) in areas of conflict such as the former Yugoslavia. The Department of State operates the Foreign Service Institute (FSI) in Arlington, Virginia, to train Foreign Service officers. FSI is one of three organizations assigned to conduct training under PDD-56.

The Department of State operates embassies abroad, headed by ambassadors whose staffs normally include representatives from other agencies of the government, including Agriculture, Commerce, Defense, Justice, and USAID. In the country team concept, the ambassador has broad responsibility for overseeing and coordinating all activities of the U.S. government within his geographic area of responsibility.

U.S. Agency for International Development

USAID is an independent agency that operates under direction of the Department of State. USAID manages programs under the Foreign Assistance Act of 1961 and similar laws. Its staff develops assistance programs, channels their funding, and oversees their accomplishment. USAID is heavily involved in assistance to the locales of complex contingency operations. The administrator of USAID is designated as Special Coordinator for International Disaster Assistance. He accomplishes this function through the Office of Foreign Disaster Assistance (OFDA). OFDA may dispatch a Disaster Assistance Response Team (DART) to assess need and help coordinate the immediate response, normally under direction of the U.S. ambassador. USAID donates U.S. agricultural commodities to meet humanitarian needs (Title II, Public Law 480). It makes these donations under government-to-government agreements, through public and private agencies, such as the World Food Programme. It also provides government-to-government grants to support long-term development (Title III, Public Law 480).

U.S. Information Agency

U.S. Information Agency (USIA) is an independent agency due to come under the Department of State in the near future. USIA presents U.S. policies to foreign audiences and advises U.S. officials concerning foreign opinion. It operates the Voice of America and other broadcasting services, manages Fulbright Scholarships, and sponsors academic exchange programs. It provides public affairs officers to U.S. embassies abroad. Its office of Research and Media Reaction assesses foreign attitudes concerning issues that affect U.S. policy and produces summaries of foreign media coverage. For example, USIA sponsors quarterly public opinion surveys in Bosnia to gauge attitudes concerning implementation of the Dayton Agreement. USIA maintains liaison with U.S. Army psychological operations (PSYOPS) units, but they normally mount separate operations with minimal coordination.

DEFENSE

Department of Defense

The National Security Act of 1947 established the Department of Defense (DoD) to draw together the armed services, including the newly established Air Force. The President and the Secretary of Defense or their representatives constitute the National Command Authority (NCA) with command over forces of the armed services. The department includes the Office of the Secretary of Defense, the Joint Chiefs of Staff, the Joint Staff, the military departments, and the combatant commands.

Military Departments

Civilian secretaries head the military departments. Through the military chiefs, these secretaries control forces not assigned to combatant commands. The military departments organize, equip, train, and supply forces but do not normally control them operationally. They are controlled operationally by unified commanders and commanders of joint task forces.

Joint Chiefs of Staff

The Joint Chiefs of Staff are the chiefs of the armed services headed by the CJCS, who is the principal military advisor to the NCA. Since the Goldwater-Nichols DoD Reorganization Act of 1986, the Joint Staff assists the CJCS who has broad responsibility for development of national military strategy and unified action of the armed forces. Within the Joint Staff, the Director for Strategic Plans and Policy (J-5) takes responsibility for military planning in peacetime. He normally prepares the plan mandated by PDD-56 and oversees its implementation. For example, the J-5 provides a representative to interagency meetings that concern Bosnia.

Unified Commands

A Unified Command Plan (UCP) establishes missions, responsibilities, and areas of responsibility for unified commands. Some unified commands are functionally organized (e.g., U.S. Transportation Command) and some are responsible for geographic areas (e.g., U.S. European Command). The reporting channel for unified commanders runs through the Joint Staff and the Chairman, Joint Chiefs of Staff, to the NCA, but they may coordinate at lower levels. For example, the commander in chief, U.S. European Command, currently coordinates directly with the Special Representative for Bosnia.

Each unified command has service components (e.g., U.S. Army Europe) and at least some forces assigned in peacetime. During conflict and war, the NCA assigns additional forces, normally according to previously prepared plans. U.S. Special Operations Command has a role analogous to an armed service to train and equip special operations forces.

Several commanders in chief of unified commands also lead international military organizations:

- Commander in Chief, U.S. European Command, always an Army general, is also Supreme Allied Commander Europe (SACEUR) within the NATO structure. While he remains, of course, under command of the U.S. President, he is also responsible to the North Atlantic Council (NAC) and as SACEUR carries out its decisions.

- Commander in Chief, U.S. Atlantic Command, always a Navy admiral, is also Supreme Allied Commander Atlantic within the NATO structure.

- Commander in Chief, U.S. Forces Korea (subordinate to Commander in Chief, U.S. Pacific Command), always an Army general, also heads the United Nations Command established during the Korean War. In this second capacity, he reports to the U.S. President, not to the Secretary General of the United Nations.

- Commander in Chief, U.S. Space Command, always an Air Force general, is also Commander in Chief, North American Aerospace Defense Command, that combines Canadian and U.S. efforts using an operations center in Cheyenne Mountain near Colorado Springs. In addition, he is the commander of his service's component, Air Force Space Command.

CENTRAL INTELLIGENCE AGENCY

The National Security Act of 1947 established the Central Intelligence Agency (CIA). Its head is the DCI, who is the principal intelligence advisor to the President and heads the intelligence community, including the National Security Agency (NSA), the Defense Intelligence Agency (DIA), the Bureau of Intelligence and Research (State Department), and the intelligence organizations of the armed services. The DCI coordinates assignment of tasks for all intelligence agencies and provides National Intelligence Support Teams (NIST) to combatant commands. The CIA has broad intelligence responsibilities outside the country and conducts counterintelligence inside the country in cooperation with the Federal Bureau of Investigation.

DEPARTMENT OF AGRICULTURE

The Department of Agriculture (USDA) improves U.S. agricultural income, develops foreign markets for U.S. agricultural products, and manages food aid programs abroad. It administers government-to-government sales to developing countries (Title I, Public Law 480), donates surplus commodities acquired by the Commodity Credit Corporation to developing and friendly countries, and finances sale of agricultural commodities on credit or by grant for the purpose of supporting new democracies.

DEPARTMENT OF COMMERCE

The Department of Commerce (DOC) promotes U.S. trade, seeks to increase U.S. competitiveness, acts to prevent unfair competition, and conducts research that supports both government and private sector planning. DOC, normally under guidance from the Department of State, plays a role in complex contingency operations whenever trade is involved. It funds the U.S. Foreign and Commercial Service that provides counseling to U.S. business and facilitates joint ventures. Under this program, Commerce currently maintains a representative in Sarajevo who monitors contracts issued through the World Bank and USAID. DOC works closely with USAID on programs with commercial interest and acts as liaison between U.S. companies and government. It currently manages the Central and Eastern Business Information Center, which provides commercial information on the countries of former Yugoslavia (except for Croatia). It also gives advice on privatization of the economies in former Yugoslavia and sponsors visits by officials from Bosnia.

DEPARTMENT OF ENERGY

The Department of Energy (DOE) operates the independent Federal Energy Regulatory Commission, administers national programs concerning energy, sponsors research into energy technologies, and has special responsibility for the nation's nuclear weapons programs. DOE maintains an emergency operations center and runs an Emergency Response Program to deal with nuclear accidents and terrorism. It would participate in any contingency operation that involved nuclear energy or the prospect of nuclear weapons.

DEPARTMENT OF JUSTICE

The Department of Justice (DOJ) gives legal advice to the President, investigates federal crimes, enforces federal laws, operates prisons, and assists state and local law enforcement officials. It includes the Federal Bureau of Investigation, the Drug Enforcement Administration, and the Immigration and Naturalization Service (INS). In conjunction with the Coast Guard, the INS deploys agents to interdict illegal immigration from such countries as Cuba and Haiti.

Under guidance from the Department of State and with funding through USAID, DOJ runs ICITAP. ICITAP conducts continuing programs to train and equip police in many countries of the world, especially in Latin America. Improvement is slow and laborious, implying that these programs must last years and even decades to show results. ICITAP developed the plan to reform law enforcement in Haiti and oversaw implementation in country. ICITAP was initially excluded from Bosnia because the United Nations had responsibility for the IPTF and there was no provision for bilateral arrangements. When deficiencies in the U.N. operation became apparent, ICITAP began training both IPTF personnel and indigenous police.

DEPARTMENT OF THE TREASURY

The Department of the Treasury advises on economic, financial, and tax policy; manages U.S. government finances; serves as the U.S. government's financial agent; enforces federal law; and manufactures specie. It includes the U.S. Secret Service, the U.S. Customs Service, the Bureau of Alcohol, Tobacco, and Firearms (BATF), and the Federal Law Enforcement Training Center. Treasury advises the World Bank and the International Monetary Fund. In this capacity, it helped develop the reconstruction program for Bosnia. Treasury has financial attachés in several embassies abroad, including Sarajevo. It currently operates a Bosnia Task Force to monitor technical assistance in such areas as debt management and fiscal policy and to review projects and loans. It has two U.S. citizens working under contract in the Finance Ministry of the Bosnian Federation government.

FEDERAL EMERGENCY MANAGEMENT AGENCY

The Federal Emergency Management Agency (FEMA) has responsibility to plan and coordinate federal response to emergencies and disasters. It also works closely with state and local governments. To discharge this responsibility, FEMA has identified emergency support functions and a lead agency for each function. For example, the Department of Defense is lead agency for public works and engineering and a supporting agency for all other emergency support functions.

OVERSEAS PRIVATE INVESTMENT CORPORATION

In 1971, Congress established the Overseas Private Investment Corporation (OPIC) as a self-sustaining, government-owned corporation under the Foreign Assistance Act of 1961. All valid claims arising from insurance and guarantees issued by OPIC constitute obligations on the full faith and credit of the United States. OPIC operates like a private business and has returned a profit in each year of its operation to date.

OPIC protects U.S. investors by providing insurance against currency inconvertibility, expropriation, and (since 1987) political violence. It finances overseas projects by guaranteeing loans and making direct loans to small businesses and cooperatives. It helps make equity capital available by guaranteeing long-term loans to private investment funds. OPIC programs are available in most countries of the world, including at the current time Bosnia and Herzegovina, Croatia, Haiti, and Somalia.

U.S. CONGRESS

> We're not off on some unfettered lark here. There are plenty of institutions that will hold us accountable. (Berger, 1997.)

The U.S. Congress oversees activities of the Executive Branch, often in detail, through a highly decentralized system of some 200 committees and sub-committees assisted by approximately 2,000 staff members. Each committee adopts its own rules, hires its own staff, and operates independently within its area of responsibility. When a committee wishes to take up a measure, it usually requests written comments from appropriate agencies of the Executive Branch, and these agencies may proffer comment on measures that affect conduct of their affairs. For example, in March 1998, the Secretary of State, Secretary of Defense, and Chairman of the Joint Chiefs of Staff submitted statements opposing a proposed House resolution that would have directed withdrawal of U.S. forces from Bosnia.

Several committees and their appropriate subcommittees routinely consider complex contingency operations and their implications for the federal budget, missions of the armed forces, and foreign policy. In the House of Representatives, these are the Committee on Appropriations (especially the National Security Subcommittee), the Committee on International Relations, and the Committee on National Security (formerly the Committee on Armed Services). In the Senate, the comparable committees are Appropriations, Foreign Relations, and Armed Services.

UNITED NATIONS SYSTEM

The term "United Nations" initially referred to the twenty-six countries that pledged in 1942 to continue war against the Axis powers (Germany, Italy, and Japan). The international organization with this name came into existence in late 1945. Member states include every independent country in the world except Switzerland, Taiwan (replaced in 1971 by the People's Republic of China), and Vatican City. By charter, the U.N. includes the General Assembly; the Security Council; the Economic and Social Council; the Trusteeship Council currently without responsibilities; the International Court of Justice located in The Hague, Netherlands; and the Secretariat headed by the Secretary General. In addition, the U.N. system includes a variety of specialized agencies and continuing programs.

United Nations Security Council

UNSC acts on behalf of the member states to ensure prompt and effective action for the maintenance of international peace and security (Chapter V, Article 24). It has five permanent members, the victorious great powers of World War II, and ten nonpermanent members elected by the General Assembly from regional groups. Permanent members have a veto right except when the question is procedural or they are parties to a dispute. According to the Charter (Chapter VII, Articles 45–47), the Security Council should include a Military Staff Committee composed of the chiefs of staff of the five permanent members, but this committee remains inactive. The Security Council may choose to act under Chapter VI (Pacific Settlement of Disputes) or Chapter VII (Action with Respect to Threats to the Peace, Breaches of the Peace, and Acts of Aggression). Invoking Chapter VII implies that the Security Council is willing to invoke sanctions (Article 41) or take action by air, sea, or land forces (Article 42). In recent years, most notoriously during the conflict in former Yugoslavia, parties have ignored and defied Security Council resolutions under Chapter VII. In two cases of successful enforcement (Korea and Kuwait), the UNSC authorized member states to act on its behalf.

United Nations Department of Humanitarian Affairs

The Secretary General established the United Nations Department of Humanitarian Affairs (UNDHA) in 1992 to better coordinate international response to emergencies, especially through the U.N. system (the organization was recently renamed as the U.N. Office for the Coordination of Humanitarian Affairs). UNDHA drew together in a standing committee the heads of several U.N. agencies (UNHCR, UNDP, UNICEF, WFP, WHO), the International Committee of the Red Cross (ICRC), and three umbrella organizations of humanitarian agencies. Other agencies and departments in the U.N. system and NGOs were also included when appropriate. UNDHA managed an emergency fund and coordinates consolidated appeals for funds.

Department of Peacekeeping Operations

The Under Secretary General for Peacekeeping Operations heads the DPKO. To date, three men have held this position: Marrack Goulding, Kofi Annan (the current Secretary General), and the incumbent Bernard Miyet. Peacekeeping implies that the Security Council is impartial with respect to the parties, i.e., it identifies neither aggressor nor victim of aggression. It further implies at least initial consent from the parties, i.e., willingness to help accomplish the peacekeeping mandate, however recalcitrant the parties may subsequently prove to be.

The first peacekeeping operation was the United Nations Truce Supervision Organization (UNTSO) commenced in June 1948 to oversee a truce in Palestine and is still in existence today. Peacekeeping expanded dramatically after the end of the Cold War but then declined rapidly. Of 48 peacekeeping operations, 35 began in the period 1988–1998. The largest, most ambitious operations were Second United Nations in Somalia (UNOSOM II) and United Nations Protection Force in Croatia and Bosnia and Herzegovina, both humiliating failures. From a peak of some 70,000 deployed personnel during 1993–1994, DPKO declined to less than 15,000 in 1997, including troops, civilian staff, military observers, and civilian police. Current operations are smaller, less ambitious—much as they were during the Cold War. The majority of these operations are observer missions, and only a few involve combat troops, e.g., United Nations Preventive Deployment Force (UNPREDEP) in Macedonia.

DPKO also has responsibility for Civilian Police (CIVPOL). Traditionally, the CIVPOL component of a peacekeeping operation consists of unarmed monitors. The IPTF in Bosnia, for example, is a CIVPOL operation. In recent years the CIVPOL mission has expanded to include training local police and, in the case of Haiti, limited law enforcement. DPKO lacks the resources to accomplish this expanded mission and has to rely on assistance from member states.

United Nations Food and Agricultural Organization

The United Nations Food and Agricultural Organization (FAO) includes most of the United Nations member states. It works to improve production and distribution of agricultural programs through technical assistance and exchange of information.

United Nations World Food Programme

The United Nations World Food Programme (WFP) assesses needs for food, provides food on an emergency basis during disasters and conflicts, and supplies food on a continuing basis to populations in developing countries. WFP works through local governments and NGOs, often in cooperation with UNHCR. It is supported by voluntary contributions in money, commodities, and services from member states and multilateral organizations.

World Health Organization

The World Health Organization (WHO) began in 1946 to coordinate international health work and to promote research in health. It helps develop international standards for agricultural and pharmaceutical products. It reports on outbreaks of communicable diseases and helps coordinate medical preparedness for disaster. It maintains official relationships with many NGOs in the health field.

United Nations Children's Fund

The United Nations Children's Fund (UNICEF) began in 1946 as the International Children's Emergency Fund to aid children in Europe and China. UNICEF provides immunizations, combats malnutrition, promotes family planning, provides care to women during pregnancy and childbirth, and generally supports public health. It is entirely supported by voluntary contributions from governments, foundations, corporations, and private individuals throughout the world.

United Nations High Commissioner for Refugees

In 1951, the General Assembly created the UNHCR, primarily to resettle European refugees left homeless by World War II. Under its mandate, UNHCR is humanitarian and nonpolitical. It is charged with protecting refugees from harm and helping find durable solutions to their problems. In the past, UNHCR aided primarily refugees who had crossed international borders, but it now increasingly aids internally displaced persons—for example, people driven from their homes by the recent conflict in Bosnia.

UNHCR has about 5,400 staff members, most of them in the field, and is currently concerned with 27 million people in some 140 countries of the world. UNHCR is almost entirely funded by voluntary contributions from governments, NGOs, and individuals. Its total budget is now about $1.4 billion per year. The U.S. State Department routinely relies on UNHCR for accurate data.

UNHCR is concerned with some two million displaced persons from former Yugoslavia, including 600,000 from Bosnia and Herzegovina who are now resident in other countries and 800,000 who are displaced within Bosnia and Herzegovina.[1] UNHCR currently promotes the Open Cities program, which channels aid to municipalities that demonstrate willingness to accept minority returns. The problem of minority returns is complex, involving property rights, identity documents, employment opportunities, police protection, and the presence of the Stabilization Force (SFOR) that contributes to a secure environment. Thus far, very few refugees have returned to areas now controlled by another nationality.

---

[1]Statement by Mrs. Sadako Ogata, United Nations High Commissioner for Refugees, Press Information Center, Tito Barracks, Sarajevo, April 16, 1998, as transcribed by the Stabilization Force.

United Nations High Commissioner for Human Rights

The Secretary General appoints the United Nations High Commissioner for Human Rights (UNHCHR) with approval of the General Assembly. UNHCHR promotes human rights, provides technical assistance to states that request help, and coordinates United Nations information programs in this field. UNHCHR work is founded on the Universal Declaration of Human Rights adopted by the General Assembly in 1948.

United Nations Development Programme

The United Nations Development Programme (UNDP) administers programs to help countries achieve sustainable development through a network of country offices. It draws together local officials, specialized agencies of the U.N., and NGOs. UNDP promotes good governance through its Democracy, Governance and Participation Program organized regionally. It is funded by voluntary contributions from nearly every country in the world. Its total yearly budget approaches $2 billion. Beneficiary countries absorb more than half of program costs by providing personnel, facilities, equipment, and supplies. UNDP assists refugees and displaced persons under the Dayton Agreement.

United Nations Educational, Scientific and Cultural Organization

The United Nations Educational, Scientific and Cultural Organization (UNESCO) is a voluntary association of member states in the United Nations that was formed in 1945. Its purpose is to promote collaboration in education, science, and culture to further respect for the rule of law and human rights. It currently has 186 members, of whom 177 have established National Commissions for UNESCO to advise their governments. UNESCO assesses obligatory contributions based on the scale used by the United Nations. Its annual budget is approximately $500 million with Germany, Japan, and Russia paying the largest shares. The United States was a founding member but became dissatisfied with UNESCO policy and withdrew in 1984. UNESCO assists in preservation of national monuments under the Dayton Agreement.

OTHER INTERNATIONAL ORGANIZATIONS

International Red Cross and Red Crescent Movement

The International Red Cross and Red Crescent Movement is a private organization that has attained official status through treaty, agreement, and usage. It encompasses the International Committee of the Red Cross (ICRC), the International Federation of Red Cross and Red Crescent Societies, and the affiliated societies. Its headquarters is in Switzerland, and its mandate derives from the Geneva Conventions of 1949 and two protocols signed in 1977. In addition, the ICRC assumes a broad responsibility for promoting international law concerning humane behavior. The ICRC works to secure the rights of prisoners of war, civilian internees, displaced persons, refugees, persons living under occupation, and victims of arbitrary treatment. It distributes aid to prisoners, attempts to trace missing persons, and helps organize repatriation. Funding comes from parties to the Geneva Convention, affiliated societies, private citizens, and the Swiss government.

The International Federation of Red Cross and Red Crescent Societies was organized in 1919 to promote affiliated societies and give unity to the movement. The affiliated societies render assistance within their home countries and may also have official status. For example, Congress chartered the American Red Cross in 1905 to relieve suffering caused by disasters. The Red Cross was adopted from the Swiss emblem, rather than religious practice, but many Islamic counties see it as Christian and prefer a Red Crescent. The Red Cross and Red Crescent symbolize the movement's neutrality and humanitarian concern and therefore their display should confer immunity.

World Bank

The World Bank includes the International Bank for Reconstruction and Development (IBRD), the International Development Association (IDA), and several other entities. By tradition, the World Bank's managing director is a U.S. citizen. IBRD and IDA share the same staff, but they are financially and legally distinct. IBRD was established in 1945 to finance reconstruction after World War II and is currently owned by 180 countries. To join the IBRD, countries must first belong to the IMF. Members are allocated shares reflecting their quotas in the IMF, which are based on relative economic strength. Voting rights are in turn based on shares. The United States currently holds about 17 percent of IBRD shares; the next largest shareholder is Japan, with about 6 percent. Members pay in a portion of their shares, and the remainder stays on call to meet the bank's obligations. IBRD borrows most of its loan money from capital markets and central banks. It loans only to creditworthy borrowers for projects that promise high rates of return to the countries involved. IDA loans money without interest to the world's poorest countries at the governmental level.

The World Bank works closely with such United Nations agencies as UNDP, UNICEF, and WHO, and with NGOs. It can play a key role in complex contingency operations. With regard to Bosnia, for example, the World Bank helped draft the overall Priority Reconstruction Program and designed specific programs to implement it, hosted donors' conferences, coordinated funds received from the international community, funded emergency projects from its own resources, and monitored economic conditions.

International Monetary Fund

The International Monetary Fund (IMF) has its origin in the conference held at Bretton Woods, New Hampshire, in July 1944. By tradition, the managing director of IMF is a European. Its Board of Governors is composed of ministers of finance or heads of central banks empowered to speak authoritatively for their respective countries. IMF is mandated to maintain a stable system of currency exchange among its members. It may lend money to members that have difficulty meeting their obligations but usually attaches conditions to ensure that the problems will not recur.

IMF membership is open to any country that conducts its own foreign policy[2] and is willing to adhere to the IMF charter. IMF currently has 181 members, including countries of the former Soviet Union. Membership is voluntary, and members may resign at any time. Each member contributes a quota subscription based on an IMF estimate of the country's wealth and economic performance. The United States has, of course, the largest quota, currently around 18 percent of the total. Special drawing rights and voting rights are proportionate to this quota. IMF is currently capitalized at about $200 billion, but only about half this balance is in major convertible currencies, i.e., dollar, yen, German mark, pound sterling, and French franc. In addition to its other functions, IMF provides technical assistance in public finance and central banking. In this capacity and by virtue of its international standing, IMF may assist in post-conflict reconstruction. For example, the Dayton Agreement stipulates (Annex 4, Article VII) that IMF will appoint the governor of the newly founded Central Bank of Bosnia and Herzegovina.

REGIONAL ORGANIZATIONS

North Atlantic Treaty Organization

NATO was formed in 1949 with unlimited duration. In Article 5 of the treaty, the parties agree that an armed attack on one or more of them shall be considered an attack against them all. The membership currently include fourteen European countries plus Canada and the United States. Meeting in Rome in 1991, the heads of state approved a strategic concept that recognizes that

---

[2]Foreign policy includes a country's arrangements for determining the value of its money in relation to the money of other countries and its handling of financial obligations with other countries and international bodies.

instabilities, including ethnic rivalries and territorial disputes in Eastern Europe, have become the most likely security challenges. To an increasing extent, the alliance members support "out of area" (non–Article 5) operations as evidenced by Bosnia.

The highest NATO authority is the North Atlantic Council (NAC) composed of all members on a basis of equality with an annually rotating presidency. The NAC may meet at the level of permanent representatives, foreign ministers, or heads of state. The Secretary General heads various planning groups and represents the alliance in both internal and external relations. The highest military authority within the alliance is the Military Committee composed of the senior military officer of each member, except France and Iceland. The International Military Staff acts as executive agent of the Military Committee. The alliance has two major military commands: Allied Command Europe, headed by the Supreme Allied Commander Europe (SACEUR) with headquarters in Casteau, Belgium, and the Allied Command Atlantic, headed by the Supreme Allied Commander Atlantic (SACLANT) with headquarters in Norfolk, Virginia. In the U.S. command chain, SACEUR is simultaneously the commander in chief, European Command, and SACLANT is the commander in chief, Atlantic Command. In addition to its regularly established commands, NATO may establish combined joint task forces comprising NATO and non-NATO forces as required to handle crises flexibly over a wider area.

Organization for Security and Cooperation in Europe

Organization for Security and Cooperation in Europe (OSCE) grew out of conferences dating to the early 1970s that concerned security issues in Europe. On August 1, 1975, 35 heads of state signed the Helsinki Final Act, establishing principles for behavior among these states and toward their own citizens. At the next summit meeting, held in Paris November 19–21, 1990, signatories to the Final Act created a permanent organization to promote its principles. The current name dates from a meeting held in Budapest four years later. Fifty-five states currently participate in OSCE, including all countries in Europe and the former Soviet Union, Canada, and the United States. OSCE gives early warning of conflict and facilitates consultations when conflict occurs. It also deploys unarmed monitors comparable to traditional United Nations observers. OSCE decisions are by consensus among the participating states.

Under the Dayton Agreement, the Republic of Bosnia and Herzegovina, the federation of Bosnia and Herzegovina, and the Republika Srpska requested OSCE to put in place an elections program and to supervise preparation and conduct of elections. OSCE discharges this responsibility through a Provisional Election Commission with the head of the OSCE mission as chairman. Because

OSCE has very limited means at its disposal, IFOR played a major role in electoral support during the first year after Dayton.

AD HOC ORGANIZATIONS

The conflict in Bosnia and subsequent implementation of the Dayton Agreement gave rise to several ad hoc organizations that may set precedents, especially the International Criminal Tribunal for the Former Yugoslavia.

Contact Group

During the conflict in former Yugoslavia, concerned powers formed the Contact Group to develop common policies and to promote a negotiated settlement. Members currently include France, Germany, Russia, the United Kingdom, and the United States plus Italy. Since Dayton, the Contact Group has continued to meet monthly or more frequently, normally in a European capital, and to issue communiqués expressing the sense of the meetings and calling for various actions.

International Criminal Tribunal for the Former Yugoslavia

In 1993, the UNSC established the International Criminal Tribunal for the Former Yugoslavia (ICTY) as recommended by the Co-Chairmen of the Steering Committee of the International Conference on the Former Yugoslavia. The enabling resolution (Resolution 827, February 22, 1993) invoked Chapter VII of the Charter. The Statute of the International Criminal Tribunal gives it power to prosecute persons who breached the Geneva Conventions of 1949, violated the laws or customs of war, committed genocide, or were responsible for crimes against humanity in the territory of the former Socialist Federal Republic of Yugoslavia beginning January 1, 1991. The tribunal sits in The Hague and is funded through the General Assembly of the United Nations and voluntary donations in cash and kind.

The tribunal is empowered to investigate crimes, indict suspects, and conduct trials, but it has no intrinsic power of arrest. The Dayton Agreement (Annex 4, Article 2 (8)) stipulates that all competent authorities in Bosnia and Herzegovina shall cooperate with the tribunal, but up to now the two entities (Federation of Bosnia and Herzegovina and Republika Srpska) "have done little or nothing to cooperate with the tribunal—they have neither enacted legislation nor arrested any indictees." (General Assembly, 1997.) The tribunal has working relationships with offices and agencies associated with implementation of the Dayton Agreement. The U.N.-controlled International Police Task Force provides information from its database of candidates to serve in the Bosnian police force. The NATO-controlled Stabilization Force supports missions of investigators, assists in exhumation programs, and has arrested several suspects indicted by the tribunal. Many indicted suspects remain at large, however, especially Radovan Karadzic and Ratko Mladic. For several years, France and the United States have planned special operations to capture these men, but hesitated to act, apparently from fear of reprisals (Sancton and Delafon, 1998, p. 68).

Peace Implementation Council

A high-level conference held in London on December 8–9, 1995, established a Peace Implementation Council (PIC) composed of the states, international organizations, and agencies attending the conference. It also established a Steering Board under the chairmanship of the High Representative that included representatives from Canada, France, Germany, Italy, Japan, Russia, the United Kingdom, the United States, and the European Commission. The Steering Board meets monthly and keeps the PIC informed of its activities.

High Representative

The five parties to the Dayton Agreement requested designation of a High Representative to facilitate their own efforts and to coordinate the activities of organizations involved in the civilian aspects of the peace settlement under a resolution of the UNSC (Annex 10, Article I (1)). He was to "Facilitate, as the High Representative judges necessary, the resolution of any difficulties arising in connection with civilian implementation." (Annex 10, Article II(1.d)). Supported by the PIC, the High Representative has assumed wide authority to act in cases when the parties fail to discharge their responsibilities. (See Chapter Four.)

NONGOVERNMENTAL ORGANIZATIONS

In U.N. terminology, NGOs are private associations that maintain consultative status with the Economic and Social Council. Some 1,500 NGOs currently enjoy such status, including businesses, foundations, professional associations, and voluntary groups concerned with development or humanitarian assistance. However, the term is commonly used to include all private groups engaged in humanitarian activities, whether or not they maintain this status. There are thousands of NGOs, some confined to single countries and others active regionally or globally.

NGOs are usually flexible in their operations. They generally recognize that some coordination is necessary but resist attempts to plan or control their activities. Most are highly competitive because their funding depends on observed performance. Most are highly sensitive to the concerns and preferences of their donors and sponsors. Soldiers often discover that workers in NGOs are antagonistic to soldiers, in part because they often perceive military establishments as a cause of human suffering. But in one contingency after another, the U.S. military has developed fruitful relationships with NGOs that need security and logistic support only the military can provide. Examples of NGOs include the following:

Catholic Relief Services

Catholic Relief Services (CRS) was founded in 1943 by Catholic Bishops in the United States, initially to provide aid to refugees during World War II. CRS now manages development projects worldwide under aegis of the U.S. Catholic Conference. It responds to disasters, assists refugees, distributes humanitarian aid, and supports development programs. For example, it currently manages a program in Bosnia to assist internally displaced persons.

Cooperative for Assistance and Relief Everywhere

Cooperative for Assistance and Relief Everywhere (CARE) was originally organized to aid the victims of World War II. CARE International is a federation of nationally chartered organizations with offices in Belgium. CARE currently has operations in the developing countries of Asia, Africa, and Latin America. It delivers humanitarian aid, supports agricultural development, helps provide health care, and encourages small businesses. CARE cooperates with specialized agencies of the U.N., national and local governments, and NGOs.

Medecins Sans Frontieres

Medecins Sans Frontieres (MSF), or Doctors Without Borders, is an organization of medical doctors that assists victims of natural disaster and war on a basis of absolute neutrality and impartiality. In cooperation with local authorities and specialized agencies of the U.N., MSF sends field missions to provide emergency medical care, rehabilitate health facilities, train medical personnel, and store emergency supplies.

Oxfam

Oxfam United Kingdom, originally the Oxford Committee for Famine Relief, relieves poverty and distress by providing emergency supplies, managing development projects, and helping developing countries to market goods.

Oxfam America provides disaster relief and manages development projects in Asia, Africa, and Latin America. It cooperates with the specialized agencies of the U.N. and many NGOs. It is funded by private donations and does not accept government funding.

ACHIEVING BETTER COORDINATION

Achieving better coordination can be immensely complicated and frustrating. The most serious problems are internal to the U.S. government. Civilian agencies lack interest in planning in part because they lack capability to implement plans directly. The interagency process too often fails to generate appropriate plans or even coherent strategies. Planning, especially advance planning, should help solve these problems. The United States must also consider how best to lead operations in the field, including relationships among various actors to promote harmony or at least keep them from working at cross-purposes.

ATTITUDES TOWARD PLANNING

There is gross disparity in resources between the Department of Defense and civilian agencies of the U.S. government. From within its own resources, Defense can make enormous contributions to complex contingency operations very quickly. By contrast, civilian agencies have very limited resources. As a result, Defense has an operational perspective, while the civilian agencies are administrative or managerial in their outlook. Understandably, Defense and civilian agencies have very different attitudes toward operational planning. Defense considers detailed, sophisticated planning essential, while civilian agencies with few exceptions display much less enthusiasm.

It would make little sense for civilian agencies to plan in detail activities they can only affect in the aggregate. Defense Department planning will normally be precise to a degree that would be undesirable or just spurious for civilian agencies of the U.S. government. When, for example, the Implementation Force needed to bridge the Sava River, it controlled and planned the entire process. (Spring floods disrupted this work in December 1995 and forced a few days' delay, proving again that few things happen exactly as planned.) To accomplish the same goal, a civilian agency, such as USAID, would normally finance a project to build a bridge and review its progress, thus having much looser control.

This contrast between military precision and looser civilian control—amounting at times to little more than influence—need not imply that civilian agencies cannot plan their contributions to complex contingency operations. They can plan activities within their areas of competence, allowing margins of error and recognizing uncertainties. Indeed, one benefit from planning may be early identification of uncertainties that demand hedging or branches in the plan ("What will we do if this happens?"). It does imply that military planning and civilian planning have different flavors and may be difficult to harmonize. Military planners will often want definite estimates ("How many C-141 sorties will this take?") in areas where civilian agencies can make only informed guesses. In this sense, there is an irreducible tension between military and civilian planning.

Interagency Process

The problem of better coordination at high level is an old and apparently intractable problem. Former Secretary of Defense Robert S. McNamara said this about arrangements during the Vietnam War:

> With the president, the secretaries of state and defense, the national security advisor, the chairman of the Joint Chiefs, and their associates dividing their attention over a host of complex and demanding issues, some of our short-comings—in particular, our failure to debate systematically the most fundamental issues—could have been predicted. To avoid these, we should have established a full-time team at the highest level—what Churchill called a War Cabinet—focused on Vietnam and nothing else. At a minimum, it should have included deputies of the secretaries of state and defense, the national security advisor, the chairman of the Joint Chiefs, and the CIA director. . . . Similar organizational arrangements should be established to direct all future military operations. (McNamara with VanDeMark. 1995, p. 332.)[1]

An acute critic of U.S. government behavior makes this general comment about the interagency process:

> The difficulty of getting the departments of defense and state as well as the CIA and the military to work together harmoniously towards presidential objectives is like untying the Gordian knot; even with a strong NSC staff, it is difficult and sometimes impossible. (Wilson, 1989, p. 273.)

---

[1]His "full-time team" approximates a Deputies Committee of the National Security Council.

Stages of the Process

The interagency process may go through stages corresponding to the levels of U.S. engagement. Defining these stages conceptually is helpful even if transitions between them are not entirely distinct to the participants. In broad terms, there might be these stages:

- Policy formulation: The United States is interested but does not contemplate a complex contingency operation as yet.

- Advance planning: The United States is sufficiently concerned to plan a complex contingency operation on a contingency basis.

- Final planning and preparation: The United States believes that a complex contingency operation is imminent and should prepare.

- Implementation: The United States is conducting a complex contingency operation, planned or not.

The NSC is fully capable and indeed has the formal responsibility to direct policy formulation and to oversee advance planning, as depicted in the "NSC-Centered Model" below. Depending on personalities, it may also be able to oversee final planning and preparation as set forth by PDD-56. But it is not clear that the NSC is fully capable of directing implementation without designation of some "point person," such as a Special Representative, to embody U.S. policy and provide public leadership. In the following discussion, we assume that a complex contingency has reached or passed the stage of final planning and preparation.

NSC-Centered Model

The Clinton Administration's Policy on Managing Complex Contingency Operations (PDD-56) defines a model centered on the NSC. This model reflects experience gained during the Haiti operation, in which the NSC, especially the directorate of Global Issues and Multilateral Affairs, played a central role.

PDD-56 calls on a Deputies Committee to establish an interagency working group, usually an Executive Committee, which brings together representatives of all participating agencies. Members of the Executive Committee are usually political appointees at the deputy assistant secretary level. They are held personally responsible for mission areas within the U.S. response, e.g., refugee affairs, demobilization of former belligerents' forces, electoral activities. The members develop agency plans that will be integrated into the political-military plan,[2] and they coordinate these plans with all relevant agencies. Through this process, they identify issues that require resolution at more senior levels. They present agency plans to the Deputies Committee, augmented as appropriate by agency representatives, during an interagency rehearsal and review. This rehearsal will usually reveal discrepancies or discontinuities that require change before the political-military plan is ready for execution. The Deputies Committee will normally rehearse or review plans just before an operation begins, before a subsequent phase begins, when a mission change occurs, and just prior to termination or transfer of responsibility. Figure 4.1 depicts the NSC-centered model described in PDD-56.

An NSC-centered model accords to the NSC the role prescribed by legislation:

> The function of the Council shall be to advise the President with respect to the integration of domestic, foreign, and military policies relating to the national security so as to enable the military services and the other departments and

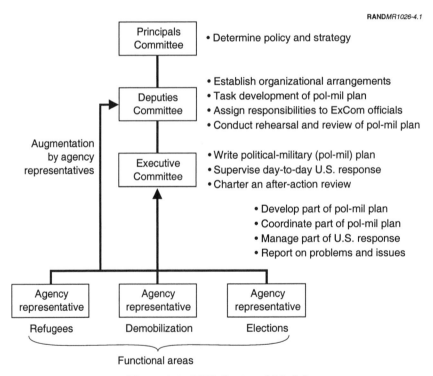

Figure 4.1—NSC-Centered Model

[2]In addition to Haiti, political-military plans have been drafted for operations in Eastern Slavonia and Kosovo. The operation in Eastern Slavonia concluded with restoration of Croatian authority. Whether an operation will be conducted in Kosovo, beyond the contemplated introduction of unarmed monitors, remains to be seen.

agencies of the Government to cooperate more effectively in matters involving the national security.[3]

It places the Assistant to the President for National Security Affairs (National Security Advisor) and his representatives in a central position where they can act as honest brokers, eliciting advice from various agencies, identifying contentious issues that must be resolved, and integrating effort in pursuit of agreed policies. This model would allow all relevant agencies to make themselves heard in meetings that encouraged open discussion, unless the National Security Advisor were to improperly use his position to stifle debate.

While attractive, an NSC-centered model also has a serious, potentially crippling disadvantage: it offers no focus for sustained personal leadership below the President, who will often be distracted by a host of competing concerns. The National Security Advisor or his representative might provide leadership, but at the risk of ceasing to be an honest broker. Even the most conscientious and candid official must have difficulty reconciling the roles of an honest broker, who encourages all views to be heard, and a leader, who can scarcely fail to promote the policy he pursues. Yet personal leadership is essential, both within Washington and in the wide world beyond. To ensure this leadership, the U.S. government has turned in practice to a quite different model.

Special Representative Model

In practice, the U.S. government has sometimes delegated exceptional powers to one individual, either informally or formally, for example as a Special Representative of the President within a particular domain. Two recent examples of such individuals are Richard Holbrooke, who facilitated an end to the Bosnian War and brokered the Dayton Agreement, and Robert S. Gelbard, who currently oversees implementation of these agreements and serves as a special envoy abroad. Both are, of course, from the Department of State, the agency that would normally bring forward individuals delegated such powers.

There would be little reason to complain about the practice of appointing Special Representatives if the normal interagency process simultaneously performed well, but it may not. Part of the motive for appointing a Special Representative may be recognition that the interagency process is working poorly, perhaps poorly enough to become a hindrance. In such circumstances, the Special Representative will have little interest in promoting the normal interagency process that he anticipates would only make his already difficult mission still harder to accomplish. He might allow or even encourage the inter-

---

[3]U.S. Code, Title 50, §402.

agency process to atrophy and coordinate directly with relevant agencies
through his department and personal staff. Figure 4.2 depicts a Special Representative model in which this shift has occurred. His staff takes overall responsibility for planning. Relevant agencies conduct most coordination through his
staff rather than through an NCA-sponsored interagency working group.

The Special Representative model gains the advantage of strong leadership at
the price of allowing the normal interagency process to atrophy. Interagency
working groups may descend to near irrelevance while the Special
Representative assumes a central role in both making and implementing policy.
When the Special Representative is an extraordinary person, there may be little
harm in this arrangement, but a system that depends critically on finding such
people is unsound and may also place too many burdens on them. Moreover, it
is doubtful whether the State Department, the normal source of Special
Representatives, can manage the interagency process as well as the NSC.

In Arnold Kanter's opinion, both logic and history argue that the NSC staff can
better manage the interagency process than can the State Department. In the
words of the Tower Commission:

> It is the National Security Advisor who has the greatest interest in making the
> national security process work. Our review of the present system and that of

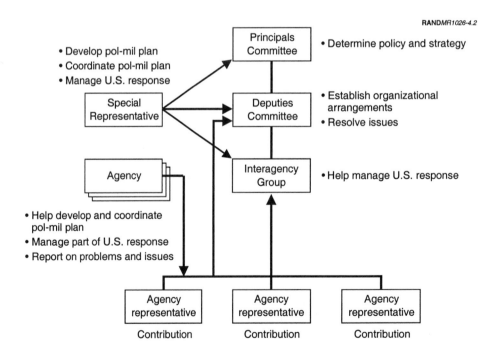

Figure 4.2—Special Representative Model

other administrations where committee chairmen came from the departments has led us to the conclusion that the present system operates better when the committees are chaired by the individual with the greatest stake in making the NSC system work. (Inderfurth and Johnson, 1998, pp. 350–351.)

The State Department's qualifications to be an honest broker among the agencies are suspect because it will normally be, and of course should be, an interested and active participant, vigorously promoting its own policy preferences.

Combined Model

A third model would combine the desirable features of an NSC-centered model and a Special Representative model. It would recognize an important role for an individual who enjoys the President's confidence but retain the interagency process outlined in PDD-56.

In a combined model, a Special Representative would implement U.S. policy and also participate in its development. With regard to its development, he might often take the lead in raising difficult issues for resolution. But his primary focus would be on implementation of policy, both domestically and abroad. He would negotiate personally or oversee negotiation within the area of his mandate. He would promote and defend policy before Congressional committees and in less formal contacts with Congressional leadership. His staff would clear public statements of policy, ensuring that the U.S. government spoke with one voice on contentious issues. Of course, he and his representatives would participate in meetings at all levels from an interagency working group, such as an Executive Committee, to meetings of the Principals Committee. But at the same time, the National Security Advisor and his representatives would oversee an interagency process centered on the NSC. Figure 4.3 depicts a model that combines a Special Representative with the interagency process described in PDD-56.

An obvious objection to this model is that it would produce tension between the Special Representative and his staff on the one side and the National Security Advisor and his staff on the other. A person with the leadership qualities required in a Special Representative is certain to have strong opinions and to promote them. Such tension might indeed occur, but it does not seem inevitable. A Special Representative will almost invariably come from the State Department and promote the State Department position. Indeed, there would be something seriously amiss if the State Department and a Special Representative drawn from the State Department were to diverge on policy, but the State Department is present at every level of the interagency process. State

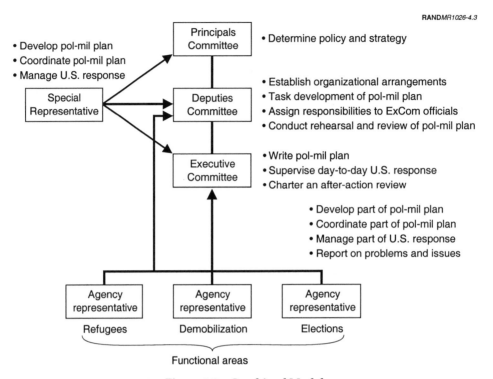

RAND*MR1026-4.3*

Figure 4.3—Combined Model

should be able to defend its position through the interagency process without any additional help from a Special Representative whose primary focus is implementation.

Evaluating the Models

If the third model is workable, it should be superior to the others because it combines their advantages. Even so, an evaluation is useful to explore desiderata for an interagency process. What should the Executive Branch expect from it?

At the outset, an interagency process should inform U.S. officials in relevant agencies about situations that threaten to produce crises that would affect U.S. interests. Some officials, especially those in regional bureaus, will be painfully aware of threatening situations, but others may lack information or be unaware of some implications. Next, the process should help familiarize officials with the capabilities and limitations of agencies other than their own. It is particularly important to bridge the civilian-military divide by informing officials in other agencies about the Defense Department, while letting Defense officials know what they can and cannot expect from other agencies.

A fundamental benefit of any interagency process is to elicit well-considered advice. Each agency in the process has its own expertise and its own outlook on the situation. Preferably at an early stage, the relevant agencies should articulate their positions in a frank and open manner. Usually these positions will be at least compatible and a broad consensus will emerge. Serious disagreements should raise important policy issues that require resolution, perhaps at the highest level. A sound interagency process should spur resolution and minimize opportunities to defer or circumvent issues that need to be resolved. During both the planning and execution of complex contingency operations, the interagency process should help integrate U.S. efforts by providing channels of communication among relevant agencies from the working level to the highest level. In addition, it should help harmonize U.S. efforts with efforts by non-U.S. agencies including international organizations and NGOs.

Finally, an interagency process should not only accommodate, but also promote, strong, continuous leadership, including leadership by people exclusively concerned with a particular contingency. Without such leadership, an interagency process may drift or cause endless bickering in Washington. Leadership is just as important abroad. Foreign officials are usually sophisticated enough to know that U.S. government includes disparate elements and will recognize differences in tone, much more substance. To make its full influence felt, the United States must be able to confront foreign officials, especially former belligerents, with a person who speaks for the United States and who cannot be circumvented or undermined. Table 4.1 evaluates the three models against the criteria. "High" implies that the criterion is fully satisfied, "Medium" that it is partially satisfied, and "Low" that it is not satisfied.

The third model is superior to the other two because it combines a robust, NSC-managed interagency process with a person wielding the extraordinary powers of a Special Representative. It should be the model of choice for complex contingency operations on the scale of Somalia, Haiti, or Bosnia. Rightly applied, the elements in this third model should complement, not thwart, each other. A Special Representative should benefit, as the President does, from an interagency process that welcomes differences of opinion until a decision is reached and then expects agencies to close ranks. The NSC should benefit from a Special Representative who implements the policy choices reached and supported through a rigorous interagency process.

Table 4.1

Criteria to Evaluate Models

Criteria	NSC-Centered Model	Special Representative Model	Combined Model
Inform U.S. officials across agencies about emerging threats.	High	Medium	High
Familiarize U.S. officials with capabilities of other agencies.	High	Medium	High
Elicit well-considered advice from U.S. agencies.	High	Low	High
Raise policy issues that require consideration.	High	Medium	High
Spur resolution of policy issues at appropriate levels.	Medium	High	High
Integrate U.S. efforts during planning and execution.	High	Medium	High
Harmonize U.S. efforts with non-U.S. efforts.	Medium	High	High
Promote strong, continuous leadership of U.S. response.	Low	High	High

PLANNING

Need for Advance Planning

PDD-56 does not specify when planning should occur, whether in advance, when a crisis is imminent, or while a crisis is in progress. However, the associated *Handbook* (Office of the Assistant Secretary of Defense, 1998) posits that a crisis is imminent or in progress. After outlining "Functions of the interagency process," the *Handbook* goes immediately to "Interagency operations during crisis" and does not discuss advance planning. This perspective is natural because PDD-56 was derived from the Haiti experience that featured a slowly developing crisis that allowed ample time for planning. The crisis grew acute on October 11, 1993, when the USS *Harlan County* was turned away by demonstrators from Port-au-Prince. Military planning was in progress by April 1994, when Secretary of Defense William Perry became involved (Hayes and Wheatley, 1995, p. 13). It became more intense during May, when U.S. Atlantic Command initiated development of a formal operational plan to forcibly remove the military junta from power. Interagency working groups began to meet during July. On July 31, the UNSC passed Resolution 940 authorizing member states to use all necessary means to facilitate departure of the military leadership. The intervention began September 19, when the Multinational Force, consisting primarily of U.S. forces, entered Haiti. Thus, the military planning process lasted five and a half months, while the interagency planning process lasted two and a half months. Figure 4.4 depicts schematically the time

RAND*MR1026-4.4*

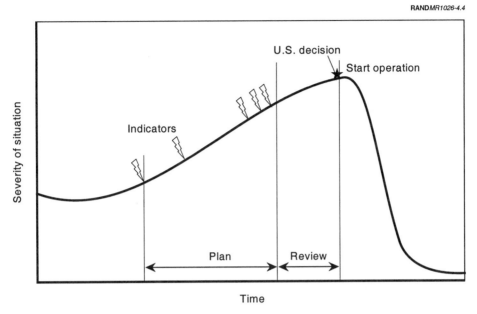

Figure 4.4—Haiti-Like Scenario

available to plan and to review plans during a scenario that resembles Haiti in 1993–1994.

In a scenario of this sort, the situation is so severe that U.S. intervention seems first likely and then inescapable well before it actually occurs. There are indicators of crisis (e.g., violations of human rights, refusals to negotiate, refugee flows) that awaken concern, but no single event that compels an immediate response. The crisis develops in a deliberate fashion, and the United States can choose the time to intervene. As a result, the United States has ample time for a deliberate process of planning and review. The Haiti scenario had all these features, but they are unlikely to all appear again in the future.

In a more-likely scenario, the situation might oscillate in severity, creating uncertainty as to whether an operation will be necessary or not. A crisis would start suddenly and escalate quickly to an event that triggered response. Figure 4.5 depicts schematically the time available to plan and to review plans during a scenario of this kind.

In a scenario of this kind, the United States would have very little time to plan and to review plans if it waited for indicators of an impending crisis. Moreover, its response might be triggered by some catastrophic or pivotal event that was

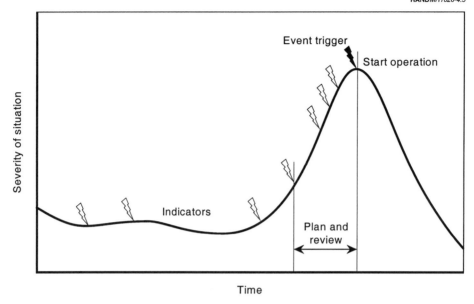

RAND*MR1026-4.5*

Figure 4.5—More-Likely Scenario

not controllable or predictable. Under such conditions, the planning process would be ragged and incomplete. Even the U.S. military can have difficulty planning its actions on short notice, especially when allied contingents are involved. Civilian agencies have far greater difficulty because they are less accustomed to planning and because during a crisis senior officials are too pre-occupied.

The obvious solution is to conduct advance planning before a crisis begins. The NSC might chair an interagency working group to review the state of the world and select those areas where complex contingencies are most likely to arise. Then the Deputies Committee might initiate advance planning for a limited number, perhaps two or three, such contingencies. Figure 4.6 superimposes an advance planning process on the schematic drawing of a more-likely scenario.

Advance planning may be the only way to achieve the sophisticated and fairly detailed planning envisioned in PDD-56, but there are obstacles and even drawbacks to such a process. An initial obstacle is indifference and skepticism about the utility of planning. The U.S. government has never planned and exe-cuted a complex contingency operation as envisioned in PDD-56 with the exception of Haiti. But barely a year after intervention in Haiti, the U.S. gov-ernment practically ignored this vision while preparing for operations in Bos-

RANDMR1026-4.6

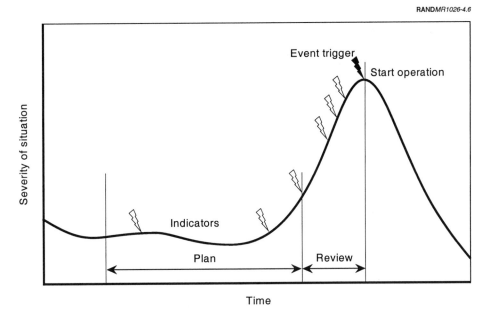

Figure 4.6—More-Likely Scenario with Advance Planning

nia. Understandably, many U.S. officials, even some highly sympathetic to planning, doubt that PDD-56 will ever be fully implemented or outlive the current administration. Therefore, it would take energetic leadership in the NSC and high-level support in key agencies to make advance planning feasible.

Another obstacle is lack of confidentiality in U.S. government circles. It is usually possible to keep the details of military planning confidential, if not the broad outlines of military planning. But most other planning, including even details of cabinet-level meetings, may leak to the press. Successive administrations have tried and failed to achieve more confidentiality. Divulging confidential information, usually for political or bureaucratic advantage, has become ingrained in Washington culture and occurs at every level of government. But the damaging effect of such leaks is a strong motive to avoid advance planning, especially for contingency operations that will be contentious, as all have been to date.

Finally, some may argue that advance planning is not feasible because the United States cannot anticipate where crises might arise. On the surface, this argument appears plausible. Who, for example, would have imagined, much less predicted, that the United States would conduct operations to end feuding and rebuild government in Somalia? Who foresaw that the Bosnian War would end when it did with a long-delayed NATO airstrike and successful Croatian offensive or that the U.S. government would commit itself to achieving a multi-ethnic state on the ruins of a four-year war? But the world is not so quirky or opaque as to obviate the utility of advance planning. Indeed, it is fairly easy to foresee where operations might be required, assuming that U.S. policy is rational and intended to advance U.S. interests.

Anticipating Crises

A simple exercise should demonstrate that the United States could predict where crises are likely and, more important, identify the crises that would probably require U.S. response. Table 4.2 lists examples of some potential crises around the globe.

This list includes only those crises that are prima facie candidates for complex contingency operations in which the United States would likely play a strong role. It omits crises that will eventually have peaceful resolutions, such as the long smoldering dispute between Quebec and English-speaking Canada. It does not include Cambodia because the United States would be unlikely to conduct large-scale operations there for historical reasons. Nor does it include such countries as Angola and Morocco where international organizations now conduct peacekeeping operations but large-scale U.S. involvement would be unlikely. Admittedly, it is not always possible to predict where the United States may decide to operate. This set is incomplete because it does not include such flukes as Somalia, where the United States chose to stay involved despite having almost no discernible interest. The next step is to devise criteria to select those potential crises that merit advance planning. It is impractical and unnecessary

Table 4.2

Examples of Potential Crises

Western Hemisphere	Middle East
Cuba (civil conflict)	Iraq (civil conflict, disintegration, threat of invasion)
Mexico (insurgency)	
Colombia (insurgency, drug traffic)	Saudi Arabia (civil conflict, threat of invasion)
	Lebanon (civil conflict, threat of invasion)
Europe	
Kosovo (insurgency, "ethnic cleansing")	**Asia**
Macedonia (disintegration)	North Korea (political and economic collapse)
Cyprus (national conflict, rivalry between Greece and Turkey)	Kashmir (insurgency, rivalry between India and Pakistan)
Africa	Indonesia (economic collapse, disintegration, civil conflict)
Algeria (insurgency)	
Burundi (ethnic conflict, genocide)	

to plan for every contingency worldwide, but the United States can and should plan for two or three contingencies that satisfy these criteria:

- The United States may not be able to prevent a crisis from occurring.

- A crisis would cause suffering and violation of human rights.

- A crisis would affect vital or important U.S. interests.

- The United States could muster political support at home and abroad for a complex contingency operation.

- The United States and others would provide enough resources to ensure success.

The first criterion is intended to winnow out those situations that the United States can expect to master through preventive diplomacy and other early actions. The second criterion identifies triggering mechanisms, the shocks to conscience that spur the United States and other countries to act. The third criterion is the most difficult to apply, but also the sine qua non. If vital or important U.S. interests are not affected, then even the administration may lose heart in the face of even minor setbacks. Applying the fourth criterion requires political judgments, especially of an administration's leadership potential. Domestic and international support depends critically on an administration's ability to convince friends that it has a sound strategy and is determined. The final criterion is the bottom line: Are the United States and its friends able and willing to pay the costs over time?

Applying these simple criteria to actual cases would certainly generate controversy. Some judgments might be easily rendered. For example, the U.S has almost no discernible interest in Burundi, and it would have difficulty mustering support for an operation in that country. During the recent Rwanda crisis, the United States and other nations, except France, showed unwillingness to undertake another large-scale operation in central Africa, even to stop genocide. But other judgments would be much harder to make. What, for example, should the United States do about rebellion in Kosovo? The United States has no direct interest in the province, but conflict that spilled from Kosovo into Albania and Macedonia could discredit and even disrupt NATO, whose continued strength is a vital interest. Figure 4.7 applies the criteria in an illustrative way without pretending to pass final judgments.

The second criterion describes not only a usual trigger, but also a fundamental rationale for action. The United States is a country founded on principles expressed in its Declaration of Independence, its Constitution, the Gettysburg

RAND*MR1026-4.7*

	Cuba	Mexico	Colombia	Kosovo	Macedonia	Cyprus	Algeria	Burundi	Iraq	Saudi Arabia	Lebanon	North Korea	Kashmir	Indonesia
U.S. may not be able to prevent a crisis from occurring	X	X	X	X	X	X	X	X	X	X	X	X	X	X
Crisis would challenge U.S. values	X	X	X	X	X	X	X	X	X	X	X	X	X	X
Crisis would affect vital or important U.S. interests	X	X	?	X	X	X			X	X	X	X	X	X
U.S. could muster political support at home and abroad	X	X	?	?	?	X			?	?	?	X	?	
U.S. and others would provide enough resources	X	?	?	?	?	X			?	?		?	?	

NOTE: Entries are illustrative.

Figure 4.7—Evaluating Possible Crises Against Criteria

Address, the Atlantic Charter of 1941, and also the Charter of the United Nations that was shaped by Americans and draws on these sources. Americans believe that their country has a unique mission to champion democracy and to defend human rights, absolutely at home and to a considerable extent abroad. Most are not particularly moved by geopolitical arguments, but they respond strongly to arguments based on America's fundamental values.

American principles are universal and undifferentiated. The Declaration of Independence says, "all men are created equal" and they have "certain unalienable rights" without any distinctions. But even the United States is not powerful enough to act consistently on universal principles and consequently must choose when to intervene and when to withhold its hand. In making these decisions, the United States consults its own interests and in this sense behaves like other countries that are less powerful or less principled. What U.S. interests might be affected? Figure 4.8 expands the second criterion[4] and evaluates the same list of possible crises against it. Again, the evaluations are illustrative.

---

[4]The list of vital and important U.S. interests is based on work by RAND colleague Stephen T. Hosmer.

RAND*MR1026-4.8*

	Cuba	Mexico	Colombia	Kosovo	Macedonia	Cyprus	Algeria	Burundi	Iraq	Saudi Arabia	Lebanon	North Korea	Kashmir	Indonesia
Endanger U.S. allies and friends				X	X	X			X	X	X	X		X
Hazard U.S. citizens living abroad		X	X							X				
Threaten use or proliferation of WMD									X			X	X	
Generate flows of refugees across U.S. borders	X	X												
Cause risk to U.S. prosperity		X				X			X	X		X		

NOTES: Entries are illustrative. Shaded areas indicate prime candidates for advance planning.

Figure 4.8—Evaluating Possible Crises Against U.S. Interests

The first of these criteria reflects America's status as a world power with allies and friends on every continent. The second reflects a consistent concern in every administration to protect U.S. citizens abroad. Weapons of mass destruction have not yet played a role in complex contingency operations but may very well do so in the future. Refugees were critically important in prompting U.S. interest in Haiti and an eventual contingency operation. Risks to U.S. prosperity are infinitely variable, but they are present in much higher degree in some areas of the world than they are in others. The entries are illustrative as before, hardly better than guesses, but if they come close to the mark, then four candidates stand out: Mexico, Iraq, Saudi Arabia, and North Korea.

This analysis shows that the U.S. government could generate a useful short list of crises that merit advance planning. Quite likely, one or more of these imagined crises would occur, fully justifying the modest effort that went into advance planning. Even if none of them occurred or the United States never responded, advance planning would have been prudent.

Front End of Advance Planning

PDD-56 calls on the Deputies Committee to establish appropriate interagency working groups to assist in policy development, planning and execution of complex contingency operations, but it describes only planning, not policy development or execution. Before planning can begin, the U.S. government must develop a policy, or more precisely a strategy, which the plan is intended to further. Otherwise, interagency working groups could only guess at strategy and might guess wrong.

On the military side, an elaborate process precedes the development of operational plans by the combatant commanders. The Chairman of the Joint Chiefs of Staff, supported by the Joint Staff (J-5), the services, and the combatant commanders, conducts a Joint Strategy Review that raises issues at the strategic and operational levels. On the basis of this work, the CJCS drafts a National Military Strategy (NMS) that is reviewed by the National Command Authority. NMS includes an appraisal of defense policy, intelligence assessment of threats to national security, strategy to achieve security objectives, and recommended force levels. In support of this strategy, the Secretary of Defense issues Defense Planning Guidance (DPG) that sets forth strategy and outlines program planning objectives that guide service budgets. On the basis of these documents, the Chairman of the Joint Chiefs of Staff issues the Joint Strategic Capabilities Plan (JSCP) that contains planning guidance to the combatant commanders. JSCP assigns missions to the combatant commanders, apportions forces and strategic lift, and directs development of plans. Combatant commanders develop highly detailed operational plans that include, for example, timed arrival of units in theater and much less detailed conceptual plans that include only generic force lists.

Planning for complex contingencies might be linked to the military's deliberate planning cycle. In the context of the NMS, the NCA could identify a small number of potential crises that would merit planning not just of military operations, but of civilian-military operations, and it could request development of plans. An interagency working group at the NSC could oversee development of agency plans and their integration. For these contingencies, the military's plans would cease to be stand-alone documents and become instead parts of larger political-military plans. In military terminology, the military parts would usually be conceptual plans that sketched broadly the objectives, concepts of operation, and required forces. Although such a planning process appears logical, it would probably provoke too much opposition and even resentment to be practical. Civilian agencies would perceive such a planning process as unwarranted militarization of U.S. policy and even an implied subordination to the Department of Defense.

In a more modest and practical scheme, the NSC might initiate advance planning on its own initiative without reference to the military's deliberate planning cycle. It could identify two or three potential crises that merited advance planning and initiate an instruction to start the process. Early in the process, it would have to promote development of strategies that would provide a sound basis for planning, implying that they should be carefully weighed and approved at principals' level. One such scheme envisions these four steps:

- Instruction for Advance Planning

- Pol-Mil Staff Estimate

- Policy Options Paper

- U.S. Strategic Approach. (NSC, 1998a.)

An interagency working group, probably a Steering Group, would accomplish the first three steps. A Deputies Committee or Principals Committee would accomplish the fourth step, after which, detailed planning could commence. The Instruction for Advance Planning would outline potential crises, U.S. purpose, scope of effort, and information requirements. The Pol-Mil Staff Estimate would assess situation and tasks, analyze planning considerations, and identify leading policy issues. The Policy Options Paper would clarify planning considerations, set goals, identify early actions, and present leading policy issues. Finally, the U.S. Strategic Approach would confirm strategic purpose, define political-military objectives, and outline an approach, including core strategy, preventive actions, crisis response, and hedging strategy.

However it is organized, the front end of advance planning should analyze the problem, develop options, and produce a strategy. To analyze the problem requires at least a midlevel interagency effort strongly supported by the intelligence community. The analysis should be reasonably comprehensive to include the most-likely scenarios and alternative strategies for handling them. But the resulting product might be fairly short, say 20 to 30 pages of closely reasoned prose with references to supporting documents. On the basis of this analysis, an interagency working group should develop options and raise the salient policy issues. For any given option, these issues might be political (should we seek a Security Council resolution?), military (should we contribute land forces?), etc. The resulting product, intended for highest-level use, would have to be succinct, say three to five pages.

The front end of advance planning should be iterative with considerable redundancy to pose the hard questions at this time, rather than later in the process. Complex contingency operations usually involve dilemmas, i.e., choices among courses of action that all seem undesirable. The United States does not seek opportunities to conduct such operations; it would rather avoid them or at least limit its participation. But U.S. leadership may be required for success and half-measures may be worse than no action at all. In various ways, Somalia, Haiti, and Bosnia all presented dilemmas to U.S. decisionmakers. Leadership at the highest level must wrestle with dilemmas, make at least tentative choices, and communicate a strategic vision so that the interagency process can take the first step to realizing this vision: development of political-military plans.

Political-Military Plans

PDD-56 envisions that an Executive Committee composed of political appointees from relevant agencies will develop a political-military plan.[5] Each of these officials will take personal responsibility for writing his part of the plan, coordinating it with relevant agencies, presenting it for review by the Deputies Committee, and ensuring its implementation if the plan is executed. A political-military plan might include a situation assessment, statement of U.S. interests, mission statement, objectives, desired end state, concept of operation, lead agency responsibilities, transition or exit strategy, organizational concept (authorities and reporting channels), preparatory tasks (accomplished before the operation begins), and mission areas (e.g., political mediation, military support, demobilization, police reform). (See Appendix B.)

Building on PDD-56, the NSC has developed a generic political-military plan in considerable detail (NSC, 1998c). It contains six sections: Situation Assessment; U.S. Interests; Strategic Purpose and Mission; Concept of Operations, Organization, and Authority; Preparatory Tasks; and Major Mission Area Tasks; These six aid development of Agency Plans. Agency Plans relate directly to major mission areas, and each is organized roughly analogous to the political-military plan as a whole.

After-Action Review

PDD-56 directs the Executive Committee to charter an after-action review that involves both those who participated in an operation and those who monitored its execution. The purpose is to capture lessons learned and to disseminate these lessons to relevant agencies. There have been no official interagency after-action reviews yet (Office of the Assistant Secretary of Defense, 1998, p. I–19). However, the Somalia experience yielded lessons that were disseminated in PDD-25 and PDD-56.

The terms "after-action" and "lessons learned" are borrowed from military practice. Subsequent to a military operation, the executing commands nor-

---

[5]See Appendix B for an outline of a generic political-military plan.

mally prepare after-action reports that outline the course of the operation, identify difficulties, and recommend improvements—the lessons learned. After-action reports typically describe the operation as a whole in glowing terms but then are extremely candid in identifying difficulties. Junior and mid-level officers, i.e., those most directly affected, usually compose the individual entries. They have no interest in glossing over problems or minimizing their effects. On the contrary, they would rather highlight difficulties with a view to preventing their recurrence.

Civilian agencies of the U.S. government may not be able to conduct candid reviews while major participants are still in office. Quite understandable motives, such as personal and political loyalty, may impede candor and shade judgments. If reviews are ever conducted, the responsible interagency working group should commission an independent effort to ensure candor. It might appoint a panel of experts who were not directly involved in the operation, or it might direct independent agencies to conduct the review.

FIELD OPERATIONS

The United States faces a different kind of problem in improving field operations than it does in improving the interagency process. The interagency process is not solely internal to an administration—Congress and the media also play roles—but it is internal to the United States, and outsiders cannot be blamed for its failings. In contrast, field operations involve outside agencies, often a large and colorful cast of agencies, that the United States can lead or influence, but not control. In field operations, the United States cannot impose a model of its own choosing. However, it can develop and promote sound principles while remaining flexible in execution.

Development of strategy is fundamental to effective operations in the field. When the United States articulates a coherent strategy, coordination and collaboration in the field can be fairly easy, even though the operations are very complex. Most people in the field, especially military officers and representatives of NGOs, want operations to succeed, and they will work selflessly to achieve common goals. These are people accustomed to looking beyond themselves, people who feel called to serve, whether in the nation's defense or the cause of common humanity. Given the opportunity, they will make convoluted, balky arrangements work or else subvert them to find a modus vivendi, but they cannot overcome lack of strategic vision at higher levels.

Lessons from Somalia

Restore Hope[6] had its origin on November 25, 1992, when the United States informed the Secretary General that it was willing to lead an operation to secure humanitarian assistance in Somalia, a country still gripped by famine caused largely by interminable clan warfare. During this operation, the United States controlled practically all the military forces in country through a Unified Task Force (UNITAF), built around the 7th Marine Expeditionary Brigade and elements of the 10th Mountain Division. As Special Envoy, Ambassador Robert B. Oakley preceded U.S. forces and negotiated agreements with clan leaders made fearful by the sudden appearance of the world's foremost military power. Meeting in Addis Ababa, Ethiopia, on January 15, 1993, the clan leaders concluded a General Agreement comprehensive disarmament, including a provision to place heavy weapons under control of international monitors. Secretary General Boutros Boutros-Ghali pressed the United States to enforce this agreement, but the new U.S. administration, like its predecessor, restricted the mission to securing humanitarian aid, while permitting its forces to accomplish some disarmament. This ambivalence kept UNITAF from being fully effective and eventually thrust UNOSOM II into an impossible situation.

During Restore Hope, Somalia provided useful experience in civilian-military collaboration, especially concerning use of a Civil-Military Operations Center (CMOC). Several NGOs had remained in Somalia during the UNOSOM I period, including the ICRC, Doctors Without Borders, and Save the Children (Seiple, 1996, pp. 97–138).[7] When the 7th Marine Expeditionary Brigade arrived in December 1992, it quickly established a CMOC collocated with the Humanitarian Operations Center (HOC) established by the U.N. The director of this center was Dr. Phillip Johnson, President of Cooperative for Assistance and Relief Everywhere (CARE). Johnson had two deputies, a civilian who headed the Disaster Assistance Response Team (DART) and a colonel from the Operations (G-3) section of 1st Marine Expeditionary Force (MEF) headquarters. HOC was a forum to exchange information, reach consensus on common approaches, and generate requests for military support, usually for convoy security. CMOC provided liaison between humanitarian agencies and UNITAF, validated requests for military support, and monitored activity in the three regional HOCs.

---

[6]Somalia involved four successive operations: First United Nations Operation in Somalia (UNOSOM I), Unified Task Force (UNITAF) designated as Restore Hope by the U.S. military, UNOSOM II with U.S. support designated as Continue Hope by the U.S. military, and UNOSOM II without U.S. support. In February 1995, the United States conducted United Shield to extract hapless UNOSOM II troops from Somalia.

[7]During the previous year, Marines had employed the CMOC concept effectively in Bangladesh during Sea Angel.

In some form or other, CMOCs are an inescapable feature of complex contingency operations. According to current joint doctrine (JCS, 1996, pp. III-16–III-19), a commander at any echelon may establish a CMOC to facilitate coordination. A CMOC provides a "meeting place" for military forces (liaison from service and functional components, liaison from other participating militaries), civilian authorities, U.S. government agencies, international organizations, NGOs, private volunteer organizations, and the population. It usually meets daily to facilitate and coordinate a wide variety of actions but especially requests from humanitarian organizations for military support.

Also during Restore Hope, Somalia provided useful experience in coordination of military operations with police activities. In an effort to provide sustainable security and to reduce direct involvement of U.S. troops in policing, UNITAF began a program of assistance to Somali police in December 1992.[8] UNITAF established an Auxiliary Security Force (ASF), composed largely of members of the former Somali National Police, as an interim step before creation of a new national police. While patrolling alone, ASF members carried only batons, but while on joint patrols with UNITAF, they carried weapons donated (under pressure) by clan leaders or provided from the weapons collection sites. The effectiveness of the ASF varied by region. It was quite effective in Mogadishu, where it enjoyed strong popular support and military support from UNITAF. It was ineffective in Kismayo because the military commander initially refused support and the local militia formed a rival group. After the firefight on October 3, the United States initiated a larger program to reestablish a national police force, but little assistance arrived before U.S. forces withdrew completely in March 1994. UNOSOM II was too weak to provide military support and also lacked sufficient resources to continue the program.

Following Restore Hope, the United States would probably have removed all military forces from Somalia had it not felt compelled to back UNOSOM II, which assumed control on March 4, 1993. Initially, the United States left one light infantry battalion as a Rapid Reaction Force. In August, as the situation continued to deteriorate, the United States deployed special operations forces and engaged in a manhunt for a Mogadishu warlord named Mohammed Farah Aideed. These special operations forces were commanded separately, adding another twist to arrangements that were already convoluted. Close personal working relationships overcame some of the problems, but they could not produce unity of command and they could not repair the lack of political will. *"[T]here should be no mistaking the fact that the greatest obstacles to unity of*

---

[8]Lynn Thomas and Steve Spataro, "Peacekeeping and Policing in Somalia," pp. 187–189, published in Robert B. Oakley, Michael J. Dziedzic, and Eliot M. Goldberg, eds., *Policing the New World Disorder: Peace Operations and Public Security*, National Defense University Press, Washington D.C., 1998. Spataro served as Provost Marshal with UNITAF.

command during UNOSOM II were imposed by the United States on itself." (Allard, 1995, p. 60.) (Emphasis in the original.) These odd arrangements are depicted in Figure 4.9.

In Somalia, the United States proved it could create cumbersome, self-defeating command relationships without help from the international community. Although nominally a U.N. operation, UNOSOM II was heavily influenced or dominated by Americans who provided the Special Representative of the Secretary General (Jonathan Howe), the Deputy Force Commander (Maj. Gen. Thomas Montgomery, USA), the commander of the Quick-Reaction Force (Montgomery again), and of course the commander of U.S. special operations forces (Maj. Gen. William Garrison, USA). Montgomery stood in an American chain of command through Central Command (CENTCOM). His forces were not part of the U.N. Forces Command, but he was dual-hatted as the Commander, U.S. Forces in Somalia, and Deputy Force Commander in UNOSOM II. As during Urgent Fury in Grenada, the special operations forces had their own unique chain of command. It became common practice for national contingents to negotiate with the U.N. Force Commander about their missions.

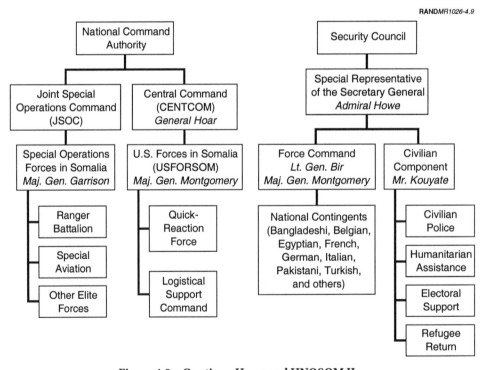

RANDMR1026-4.9

Figure 4.9—Continue Hope and UNOSOM II

As the situation worsened in Somalia, national contingents became increasingly reluctant to accept direction from the U.N. Force Commander, taking orders instead from their home governments. Even as it tried to limit its participation, the United States became more deeply involved, especially in the manhunt for Aideed. Lack of coordination became painfully obvious on October 3, 1993, when Montgomery had to scrape together Pakistani tanks and Malaysian infantry fighting vehicles to relieve Rangers pinned down by fire in Mogadishu. Eighteen Americans were killed, precipitating a policy debate. The administration decided to reinforce Montgomery's command with armored vehicles, but at the same time, it reduced his mission practically to self-defense and set a deadline for the departure of all U.S. forces. After their departure in March 1994, UNOSOM II was so ineffective that it finally required U.S. assistance even to withdraw safely.

Somalia taught these broad lessons about complex contingencies:

- Clear statement of a feasible mission, starting with the U.S. government's own statement, is fundamental to success.

- Unity of command, starting with U.S. forces, is as important in complex contingency operations as it is in war.

- During conflict, parties regard humanitarian assistance as a means to enhance their power or degrade their adversaries. Only strong military force can prevent them from diverting and misappropriating assistance.

- U.N.-controlled forces can do little more than defend themselves and should not be deployed during conflict.

- An outside military force can stop parties from fighting, but it cannot compel them to build a peaceful society.

Somalia taught these lessons more explicitly directed toward civilian-military cooperation:

- Military forces and relief agencies are highly disparate in culture, but they will collaborate willingly if provided liaison, preferably through a well-supported CMOC.

- In the absence of reliable government, no clear dividing line exists between military operations and law enforcement.

- When military forces are deployed into a turbulent situation, they cannot escape some responsibility for public order.

- The credibility of newly established police forces may depend critically on military support in emergency situations.

- The U.N. can monitor police activities, but it lacks the resources and experience required to develop new police forces.

- Developing new police forces demands long-term effort and should not be considered a quick exit strategy.

Lessons from Haiti

International Civilian Mission in Haiti (MICIVIH)[9] deployed in early 1993 to monitor human rights but was withdrawn in October when the Security Council imposed sanctions to enforce the Governors Island Accords between the military regime, and the deposed President Jean-Bertrand Aristide. After the military leaders agreed to surrender power under threat of invasion, the Multinational Force (MNF), designated Uphold Democracy, deployed to Haiti on September 19, 1994. It was a large and capable force including two brigades of the U.S. 10th Mountain Division and a Marine Expeditionary Unit. President Aristide returned on October 15 and MNF handed over to United Nations Mission in Haiti (UNMIH) on March 31 of the following year. The U.S. military contribution to UNMIH was much smaller, consisting primarily of an infantry battalion, a special operations task force, and support elements. On August 1, 1996, UNMIH was replaced by United Nations Support Mission in Haiti (UNSMIH) with U.S. participation reduced to a 500-man Support Group. On July 31, 1997, UNSMIH was renamed United Nations Transition Mission in Haiti (UNTMIH). Its mandate expired on November 30, 1997, but the United States continues to maintain a support unit in Haiti on a bilateral basis.

During the preparation phase, Haiti provided useful experience in planning complex contingency operations, which was later codified in PDD-56. Planning began in June and July 1994 when the regime headed by Raoul Cédras revealed it would not voluntarily relinquish power. It became intensive during August and early September, when some kind of U.S. military action began to appear inevitable. Richard A. Clarke, Senior Director for Global Issues and Multilateral Affairs, National Security Council, worked closely with Lt. Gen. Wesley K. Clark, USA, Director for Strategic Plans & Policy (J-5), Joint Staff, to develop plans. Clarke insisted that political appointees, normally at the assistant secretary level, be responsible for mission areas rather than for their own agencies' contributions. In other words, he made missions, not agencies, the basis for planning. This distinction is more important than it may appear. If political appointees had been responsible only for their own agencies' contributions,

---

[9]Haiti involved five operations: the International Civilian Mission in Haiti (MICIVIH), Multinational Force (MNF) designated Uphold Democracy by the U.S. military, United Nations Mission in Haiti (UNMIH) designated Restore Democracy by the U.S. military, United Nations Support Mission in Haiti (UNSMIH), and finally United Nations Transition Mission in Haiti (UNTMIH).

then they would have borne no personal responsibility for interagency coordination and could have blamed agencies other than their own for failures. Integral to the planning process was rehearsal, generally in the form of briefings, first within lead agencies and then at the Deputies' level through NSC. Rehearsals revealed which issues remained unresolved, especially in the area of interagency coordination.

The planning for Haiti revealed inherent weaknesses in the interagency process. Planning depended critically on personalities, especially on Clarke at the NSC who initiated planning through a directive and drove it to completion. But neither Clarke nor the NSC had authority to ensure that lead agencies produced their plans on schedule. The same weakness became apparent during implementation of the plan when no one seemed able and willing to hold assistant secretaries or their agencies responsible when milestones were not reached. These instances revealed essential differences between the political-military plan and a military plan. A military plan is issued under authority of a commander and is binding on his subordinates. The political-military plan did not have such characteristics. It was not issued under any particular authority and did not bind anyone. These differences were often frustrating for military officers, who were accustomed to the much greater rigor of their own organizations.

Haiti provided valuable experience in law enforcement during complex contingency operations. Initially, the Chairman of the Joint Chiefs of Staff stated: "The task of keeping law and order in Haiti is the responsibility of the Haitian police force and the Haitian military. We are not in a business of doing day-to-day law and order. . . ."[10] But it quickly proved intolerable for well-armed U.S. troops to ignore violence, and so the U.S. military assumed direct responsibility for law enforcement. By October 1994, the MNF had two U.S. military police battalions in Haiti's urban areas. These military police conducted combined patrols with the International Police Monitors and an Interim Public Security Force composed of former Haitian police and soldiers vetted by the U.S. and Haitian authorities. Coordination of military forces and civilian police became more difficult after UNMIH assumed control because the Special Representative of the Secretary General (SRSG) lacked a staff to ensure this coordination.

The Department of Justice, through ICITAP, took broad responsibility for programs to develop the Haitian police. From the outset, ICITAP saw the need to create a new National Police Force separate from the Haitian Armed Forces. (In January 1995, the returned President Aristide would disband the Haitian Armed Forces to prevent the danger of a military coup.) During May 1993, ICITAP

---

[10]Briefing, Gen. John Shalikashvili, USA, White House, September 20, 1994, Reuter.

served on a multinational working group sponsored by the United Nations to draft terms of reference for International Police Monitors (U.S. Department of Justice, 1993). Unlike any U.N. civilian police contingent in the past, these monitors were authorized to carry weapons and to enforce Haitian law. The ICITAP plan foresaw two phases: a transition phase to develop the infrastructure for a National Police Force and a phase of institution building to institutionalize the new police force.

Haiti demonstrated that military forces have broad utility and should be prepared for unforeseen tasks. Their fundamental mission was, of course, security, including the person of President Aristide, government installations, humanitarian aid convoys, polling places, and ballots. Presidential security was vital because his assassination might have jeopardized the entire mission. Military forces also accomplished unforeseen tasks. The most important was law enforcement, as previously noted. Had U.S. troops not become deeply involved in day-to-day law enforcement, they could not have established the secure environment required for transition to a U.N.-controlled operation. In addition, U.S. forces accomplished emergency repairs to essential infrastructure, including restoration of electrical power in Port-au-Prince and other urban areas. They provided emergency medical care and prepared to conduct disaster relief, especially in the wake of hurricanes.

Special operations forces, predominately the U.S. Army's Special Forces, played a prominent role in Haiti. Special Forces (SF) are organized and specially trained to operate closely with indigenous people and foreign militaries. They proved invaluable in Haiti, especially in the barely accessible interior. They typically deployed in teams of even smaller detachments and lived among the Haitians. Because of the breakdown in Haitian government, SF acquired missions that covered almost the entire spectrum of local government. During UNMIH, SF staffed Coalition Support Teams that provided liaison between foreign contingents and the Force Commander, a U.S. general officer. Also during UNMIH, SF provided a quick-reaction force deployable by air or land in support of UNMIH or Haitian police.

During Uphold Democracy, command relationships and requirements for coordination were dominated by the United States, so much so that the operation had almost the feel of an internal affair. Arrangements became more complicated and more typical of complex contingency operations when UNMIH assumed responsibility on March 31, 1995, in a ceremony attended by the U.S. President and the Secretary General of the United Nations. U.S. Atlantic Command (USACOM) prepared for this transition by hosting a six-day training session in Port-au-Prince for UNMIH civilian and military staff members. One of the Force Commander's conditions for transition from MNF to UNMIH was that 85 percent of his staff be in country and trained. The Force

Commander was a U.S. general initially exercising operational control over contingents from Bangladesh, Canada, Honduras, India, the Netherlands, Pakistan, Nepal, and Caribbean states (Antigua, Bahamas, Jamaica, and Trinidad and Tobago). He reported through U.S. channels to USACOM and through U.N. channels to the Special Representative of the Secretary General (SRSG). These arrangements are depicted in Figure 4.10.

Complex working relationships are usually required to make an operation successful. In Haiti, coordination or collaboration was required inter alia among U.N. headquarters, several U.N. programs and agencies, the American Embassy, USACOM, USAID, NGOs, and, of course, the government of Haiti (U.S. Army Peacekeeping Institute, 1996, p. 12). The SRSG, Force Commander, and Commander of the Civilian Police usually met at least once a week with President Aristide to review issues relative to the UNMIH mandate (U.N. Security Council, 1995, p. 2). In addition, the SRSG and senior UNMIH officials maintained close contact with a wide variety of Haitian officials and prominent citizens.

RANDMR1026-4.10

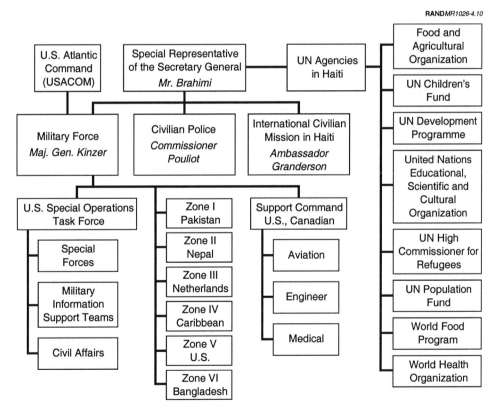

Figure 4.10—Restore Democracy and UNMIH

Haiti taught these broad lessons about complex contingencies:

- The doctrine of overwhelming force applies as much to complex contingency operations as it does to war, with the difference that the aim is to prevent combat from occurring by making resistance appear futile.

- The interagency process needs the focus and discipline provided by a common political-military plan.

- Rehearsal helps improve a political-military plan by revealing its discontinuities and synchronizing agency plans.

- An appropriate U.S. official in each agency should be held personally responsible for accomplishing each objective contained in the common plan.

- No operation stays exactly on schedule, but a sound plan makes adjustment easier.

- Smooth transfers of overall responsibility for an operation require preparation, preferably on-site training and exercise.

- Law enforcement depends on police forces, judiciary, and a penal system, institutions that may require years to develop, well beyond the span of a complex contingency operation.

Haiti taught these lessons more explicitly directed toward civilian-military cooperation:

- Military forces cannot avoid law enforcement if violence threatens to become widespread.

- There is a large potential gap between military forces, which have overwhelming strength but cannot always be present, and indigenous police forces, which are present but may not be adequate.

- When military forces and police officers, including international monitors and indigenous police, must work together, a staff should be in place to ensure their coordination.

- Especially during the initial phase of an operation, military forces may be the only ones able to accomplish urgent nonmilitary tasks, such as repair of infrastructure.

- The traditional U.N. structure centering on an SRSG is adequate for complex contingency operations in a secure environment, but it requires a spirit of teamwork and compatible personalities.

Lessons from Bosnia

To date, Bosnia[11] has involved three major operations and several subsidiary operations. The major operations were United Nations Protection Force (UNPROFOR) February 21, 1992, to December 20, 1995; NATO Operation Joint Endeavor, involving the Implementation Force (IFOR), December 5, 1995, to December 20, 1996; and NATO Operation Joint Guard, involving the Stabilization Force (SFOR), December 21, 1996, to the present. Subsidiary operations included Deny Flight (enforcement of a no-fly zone over Bosnia), April 12, 1993, to December 20, 1995; Sharp Guard (maritime enforcement of sanctions imposed against former Yugoslavia), June 15, 1993, to October 1, 1996; Deliberate Force (air strikes against Bosnian Serb targets), August 29, 1995, to September 20, 1995; and Able Sentry (observation mission in northern Macedonia), July 1, 1993, to the present.

UNPROFOR was a lightly armed peacekeeping force deployed where there was no peace to keep. Indeed, UNPROFOR was so weak that it negated NATO airpower by becoming hostage to the Bosnian Serbs. NATO offered its airpower both for close air support of UNPROFOR and to enforce U.N. declared "safe areas." The fall of one such "safe area"—Srebrenica—and subsequent massacres inspired NATO to enforce a weapons exclusion zone around Sarajevo through Deliberate Force. Several factors, including Deliberate Force, a successful Croatian offensive, general war weariness, and relentless U.S. diplomatic effort, led to the Dayton Agreement[12] that included military provisions to prevent armed conflict (Annex 1A) and civilian provisions. These latter provisions provided for two separate "entities" (Federation and Serb Republic) but also for a unified multinational state on the same territory.

During the last years of the Bosnian war, NATO developed widely disparate plans reflecting alternative policies considered in Washington and in the North Atlantic Council. On the one hand, NATO planned to enforce a zone of separation in Bosnia (Discipline Guard), while on the other it planned to secure the withdrawal of UNPROFOR (Determined Effort) (Holbrooke, 1998, pp. 65–66).[13] Military planning was thus well advanced well prior to the Dayton Conference.

---

[11]The Republic of Bosnia and Herzegovina encompasses the Federation of Bosnia and Herzegovina and the Republika Srpska (Serb Republic). For brevity, it will be referred to as "Bosnia."

[12]The General Framework Agreement for Peace in Bosnia and Herzegovina was initialed in Dayton, Ohio, on November 21, 1995, and signed in Paris on December 14, 1995, by the Republic of Bosnia and Herzegovina, the Republic of Croatia, and the Federal Republic of Yugoslavia (reduced to Serbia and Montenegro).

[13]Also see John Pomfret, "U.S. Foresees Sending GIs To Help U.N. Quit Croatia," *Washington Post*, February 25, 1995, pp. A1, A20; John F. Harris, "Clinton Vows Help for U.N. Troops in Bosnia," *Washington Post*, June 1, 1995, pp. A1, A19; Hearing of the House National Security Committee chaired by Rep. Floyd Spence (R-S.C.), June 7, 1995; Rick Atkinson, "NATO Drafts Plans for Smaller Bosnia Role," *Washington Post*, August 18, 1995, p. A33.

During Dayton, Lt. Gen. Wesley Clark, USA, helped draft the military provisions as a member of Holbrooke's team. At the same time, Clark directed U.S. military planning as the Director for Strategic Plans & Policy (J-5) on the Joint Staff. After the Dayton Conference, when the Joint Staff briefed its plan to implement Annex 1A, military officers expected to learn how the civilian departments intended to implement other annexes. They were astonished to discover that no other department had produced a plan. It appeared that no one was leading a planning effort in Washington and the State Department was at odds with itself.

Ambassador Robert L. Gallucci, who had helped compose the agreement on an international police task force (Annex 11), was expected to represent the Department of State and to lead the planning effort. But although designated Special Advisor on Bosnia Implementation, others checked Gallucci within his own department. At interagency meetings, representatives of the State Department debated among themselves while other agencies waited for a State Department position to emerge. The NSC staff was disappointed because it had expected Gallucci to lead the interagency planning process for Bosnia. Moreover, State and Defense were in strong disagreement over policy, with State favoring a more active role for military forces and Defense holding back. As a result, the administration did not produce a political-military plan and civilian-military coordination was poor. During the critical months following Dayton, no one in Washington adequately planned how the High Representative would relate to IFOR, how the International Police Task Force (IPTF) would operate, or how reconstruction would be financed.

The Dayton Agreement reflected the complex nature of the settlement. At Dayton, the parties agreed that a NATO-controlled IFOR would have the right to coerce them. Dayton delineated the tasks that IFOR had the right to accomplish without qualification—essentially Annex 1A—and the tasks it had the right to accomplish "within the limits of its principal tasks and available resources, and on request."[14] The latter were complex and entangling tasks, such as preventing interference with movement of refugees. Dayton invited the UNSC to adopt an enabling resolution. It accorded responsibilities associated with implementation to various international organizations. It established a High Representative "to facilitate the Parties' own efforts"[15] and to coordinate the civilian aspects of the peace settlement. In various contexts, the High Representative was empowered to monitor, maintain close contact, coordinate, facilitate, participate in meetings, and report. He was to establish liaison with IFOR, but "not in any way interfere in the conduct of military operations or the IFOR

---

[14]The General Framework Agreement for Peace in Bosnia and Herzegovina, Annex 1A, Article VI.
[15]Ibid., Annex 10, Article I.

chain of command."[16] This prohibition reflected determination to preclude the sort of dual-key arrangement that been disastrous during the UNPROFOR period. Table 4.3 summarizes roles outlined in the Dayton Agreement.

On December 8–9, an exceptionally well-attended Peace Implementation Conference was held in London. At this London Conference, the Secretary General of the United Nations announced that he would propose to the Security Council the role the U.N. would play in civilian implementation, including the International Police Task Force. The acting Secretary General of NATO and the Supreme Allied Commander Europe (SACEUR) briefed plans for deployment and employment of IFOR. Carl Bildt of Sweden, the European Union Mediator for Bosnia, soon to become High Representative, briefed the tasks involved in civilian implementation. The United Nations High Commissioner for Refugees outlined the main tasks associated with refugees and displaced persons. The President of the International Committee of the Red Cross outlined his tasks

Table 4.3

Roles Described in the Dayton Agreement

Agency	Role
UNSC	Adopt a resolution authorizing member states to establish IFOR (Annex 1A); establish an International Police Task Force (Annex 11, Article I).
UNHCHR	Monitor human rights situation in Bosnia and Herzegovina (Annex 6, Article XIII).
UNHCR	Develop a repatriation plan for return of refugees (Annex 7, Article I).
UNDP	Assist refugees and displaced persons (Annex 7, Article III).
UNESCO	Appoint two members to the Commission to Preserve National Monuments (Annex 8, Article II).
IFOR	Use necessary force to ensure compliance with certain provisions (Annex 1A).
High Representative	Facilitate parties' efforts; mobilize and coordinate activities of agencies involved in civilian aspects.
ICRC	Develop and monitor plan for release and transfer of prisoners (Annex 1A, Article IX); determine fate of persons unaccounted for (Annex 7, Article V).
OSCE	Facilitate arms control negotiations (Annex 1B); put an elections program in place (Annex 3); appoint Ombudsman for Human Rights (Annex 6, Article IV).
IMF	Appoint Governor to the Central Bank of Bosnia and Herzegovina (Annex 4, Article VII).
Council of Europe	Appoint eight members of the Human Rights Chamber (Annex 6, Article VII).

---

[16]Ibid., Annex 10, Article II.

under the peace agreement. The Secretary General of the OSCE reported its preparations to support electoral activities. The President of the World Bank outlined the bank's role in reconstruction. The President of the Council of Ministers of the European Union presented his thoughts on relations between Bosnia and the European Union. The London Conference established a Peace Implementation Council (PIC) composed of concerned states and the international organizations and agencies attending the conference and a Steering Board composed of representatives from concerned states, including Japan as a major donor.

The Dayton Agreement[17] and the London Conference[18] emphasized the need for coordination between the IFOR Commander and the High Representative but failed to establish a mechanism and in fact coordination was poor. At the outset, there was gross disparity in resources and authority between IFOR and the Office of the High Representative (OHR). IFOR was executing a long-planned military operation backed by the world's most sophisticated regional alliance, and the NATO countries were determined to execute the military operation successfully. French officers, for example, greeted the SACEUR, at that time Gen. George A. Joulwan, USA, with enthusiasm because the time of their humiliation was over. In strong contrast, the High Representative had very limited resources at his disposal, not even adequate office space. This disparity discouraged cooperation with the High Representative, who appeared headed for failure. Moreover, the policy dispute in Washington meant that the Deputy High Representative, at that time James ("Jock") Kovey, received little guidance through national channels.

Gorazde illustrated the lack of coordination. This village and its environs constituted a Muslim enclave in Bosnian Serb territory, in fact the only "safe area" in eastern Bosnia that survived the war. Not surprisingly, Bosnian Serbs detained and kidnapped Muslims in the Gorazde Corridor, a narrow road winding through wooded hills. The High Representative requested that the IFOR Commander, at that time Adm. Leighton Smith, USN, address the problem, but the IFOR Commander asserted it was an IPTF responsibility. Since the police monitors were unarmed and had no authority to enforce law, referring the problem to them meant it would not be solved. Appalled at the lack of coordination, members of both staffs suggested a coordinating mechanism, but

---

[17]"The High Representative or his designated representative shall remain in close contact with the IFOR Commander or his designated representatives and establish appropriate liaison arrangements with the IFOR Commander to facilitate the discharge of their respective responsibilities," The General Framework Agreement for Peace in Bosnia and Herzegovina, Paris, December 14, 1995, Annex 10, Article II.

[18]"The conference notes that close cooperation between IFOR, the High Representative and the agencies will be vital to ensure the success of the implementation period," conclusions of the Peace Implementation Conference held at Lancaster House, London, December 8–9, 1995, Paragraph 10.

at first neither Bildt nor Smith would approve. Finally, they put together a working group analogous to an interagency working group in U.S. practice and coordination improved. IFOR eventually provided security on the Gorazde Corridor and also rebuilt the road leading to the enclave.

IPTF was established as a CIVPOL operation. CIVPOL is a small ad hoc organization within the DPKO. It lacks resources to train and equip police monitors; it simply solicited national contingents. These officers were supposed to have five to eight years of police experience, driver's licenses, and knowledge of English, but some failed to meet even this minimal standard. Initially, there was no provision for bilateral assistance and therefore ICITAP was left out despite its valuable experience in Haiti. Some eight months into the operation, ICITAP received approval to establish a training program for newly arrived police monitors.

Early in the operation, a wide gap became apparent between the capabilities of IFOR and the IPTF. This gap was no surprise; indeed it had been anticipated at the peace conference. During the Dayton negotiations, there was a dichotomy between the Americans, who took responsibility for military implementation, and the Europeans, who accepted responsibility for civilian implementation. The U.S. Department of Defense refused to take on law enforcement, fearing that it would be open-ended, frustrating, and risky, but there was no agreement on arming the IPTF. As a result, law enforcement was left to indigenous police forces that no one trusted to enforce law fairly and effectively. Although this issue continued to provoke acrimonious debate in Washington, IFOR/SFOR and IPTF enjoyed cordial relations in Bosnia. IFOR/SFOR officers realized that they could not remain aloof if IPTF were seriously threatened. Consequently, IFOR/SFOR planned to assist if necessary but did not acknowledge such plans, because they implied involvement in law enforcement. In May 1998, the NAC approved a plan to fill this gap by creating a Multinational Security Unit (MSU) under NATO control. The initial MSU battalion included Italian carabinieri and Argentine gendarmes equipped with small arms and wearing their national uniforms (Cruger, 1998, p. 1).

When U.S. forces first entered Bosnia, the President and Secretary of Defense stated that the deployment would last one year. Although skepticism about this deadline was widespread, official planners had to assume it was meant seriously. On November 15, 1996, the President announced that U.S. troops would remain until mid-1998, but in December 1997 he decided they would remain indefinitely. Sen. John McCain (R-Ariz.) said, "I certainly hope they don't insult our intelligence again with another departure date." (Bennet, 1997, p. 1.)

In early 1997, the National Security Advisor Samuel R. ("Sandy") Berger worked to resolve the persistent disputes over policy in Bosnia and the consequent incoherence. Under his lead, the NSC conducted a policy review that led to more coherent implementation of the Dayton Agreement. In May, the President appointed Robert Gelbard his Special Representative for Bosnia. Supported by a small ad hoc staff in the State Department, Gelbard developed a plan to implement the Dayton Agreement. He avoided Gallucci's fate, and by autumn he had established himself in a leading position for formulation and execution of policy. In July, Gen. Wesley K. Clark, USA, who had served on Holbrooke's negotiating team, became SACEUR.[19] Gelbard and Clark coordinated directly with each other, imparting a new coherence to U.S. policy and greater flexibility. Together, they promoted more moderate, although nationalistic Serbs in Banja Luka over the intransigent, often thuggish faction in Pale, a major step toward implementation. On October 1, 1997, NATO troops seized four television towers in the Serb Republic that were broadcasting nationalist propaganda. On October 8, they intervened to prevent conflict between police loyal to the hard-line regime in Pale and police loyal to a more moderate regime in Banja Luka. Over the following months, they brought Serb special police within the levels allowed by Dayton and suppressed smuggling that supported the Pale regime.

While the United States implemented this more aggressive strategy, the High Representative gained power and became more assertive. On May 30, 1997, the Steering Board of the Peace Implementation Council held a pivotal meeting in Sintra, Portugal. The board found that all authorities in Bosnia were failing to live up to their obligations under the Dayton Agreement and set forth its criteria for compliance. It welcomed the new High Representative, Spanish diplomat Carlos Westendorp, and asked him to recommend "specific action to be taken by the international community in each case" of noncompliance.[20] From experience, Westendorp had a deep personal antipathy to one-party nationalist regimes cloaked in religion, the very sort of regime that all parties are perpetuating in Bosnia. In the following months, Westendorp strove for closer coordination with the SFOR. He believed that SFOR would ultimately be judged by its contribution to implementation:

> Il faut de dépêcher et profiter de la présence des troupes de l'OTAN sur place pour faire avancer la processus de paix. Le déploiement de cette force ne sera éternel. Cette présence ne se justifie aux yeux de l'opinion publique inter-

---

[19]One often hears or reads that Clark was more willing than Joulwan to help implement civilian provisions of Dayton. Possibly, but it is difficult to see how Joulwan could have taken a stronger line while U.S. policy was in such disarray.

[20]Political Declaration from Ministerial Meeting of the Steering Board of the Peace Implementation Council, Sintra, May 30, 1997, Paragraph 92.

nationale que si des résultats en découlent et que des progrès sont visibles dans la mise en place des accords de Dayton.[21]

Since his appointment, Westendorp has become involved in almost every aspect of implementation. With the backing of the Peace Implementation Council, he interpreted his mandate under Annex 10 to mean that if the parties fail to meet their obligations, the High Representative would act for them. The OHR terminated endless bickering by choosing designs for Bosnia's flag, its currency, and its license plate. It is currently at work on the national anthem. It operates an Economic Task Force and recommends who should receive international aid, based on compliance with Dayton. It operates a Return and Reconstruction Task Force that includes SFOR and United Nations Mission in Bosnia and Herzegovina (UNMIBH). It oversees creation of common institutions and development of a common legal system. It cooperates with the OSCE to ensure the proper conduct of voter registration and elections. It oversees the local media, promotes the independent Open Broadcast Network, and disseminates public information. It helps negotiate or mediate mail service, telephone service, civil aviation, and public utilities.

The World Bank, the European Bank for Reconstruction and Development (EBRD), and the European Commission devised the Priority Reconstruction Program for Bosnia with assistance from U.S. agencies, especially the State Department and Treasury. This program includes rehabilitation of existing infrastructure, rehabilitation of potential areas of refugee return designated by UNHCR, job creation through public works projects and credit for small businesses, and support for governmental institutions. With assistance from State, the World Bank hosts periodic donors' conferences where large donors pledge funds, often earmarking how these funds should be spent. Under the Eastern European Assistance Act of 1989, the United States channels $400 million to $500 million yearly through USAID to implement the Dayton Agreement. Granting and withholding aid is a very blunt instrument but has helped promote implementation, most importantly by withholding aid from Pale and then granting aid to Banja Luka. USAID initiated the Community Infrastructure Rehabilitation Program, a small program ($5 million in 1997) that allows U.S. military authorities to fund municipal projects in their areas of operation.

Even the formal relationships, let alone working relationships, among agencies implementing Dayton are too complex to be captured by an organizational

---

[21]It is necessary to dispatch and to profit from the presence of NATO troops to advance the peace process. The deployment of these troops is not eternal. This presence will not appear justified to international public opinion unless results follow and there is visible progress in implementing the Dayton Agreement. "Il faut profiter de la présence des troupes de l'OTAN pour faire avancer le processus de paix," *Le Monde*, January 27, 1998.

chart. Suggesting this complexity, four primary actors, the parties, and a selection of other agencies are depicted in Figure 4.11.

From an organizational perspective, arrangements in Bosnia look unworkable, and they would be unworkable if the primary actors were not in broad agreement. Four separate organizations, each with its own channel of communications, are responsible for four interrelated aspects of Dayton implementation:

- NATO accomplishes military tasks and supports aspects of civilian implementation, including inter alia security for the Banja Luka regime, enforcement of OHR media policy, support to IPTF, support of electoral activities, and infrastructure repair. NATO also controls the newly created Multinational Security Unit that provides emergency support to law enforcement.

- The Peace Implementation Council, through the Steering Board, gives direction to the High Representative, who monitors compliance with Dayton and acts when the parties procrastinate and are obstructive.

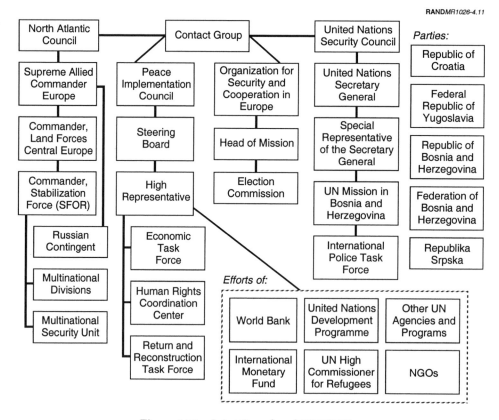

Figure 4.11—Joint Guard and UNMIBH

- The Organization for Security and Cooperation in Europe helps monitor observance of human rights, helps supervise and organize voter registration and elections, and promotes confidence-building measures among the parties.

- The UNSC controls the UNMIBH, which directs the International Police Task Force, which monitors and advises indigenous police.

Coordination of these disparate organizations is possible because certain states are present in all of them. The Contact Group, established during the conflict and continued since Dayton, is shown in a central position because it contains Britain, France, Germany, Italy, Russia, and the United States, the most important of these states. Among these states are, of course, leading members of the NAC, the Peace Implementation Council, and the OSCE, as well as all but one (China) of the permanent members of the UNSC. Viewed from this perspective, Bosnia seems designed to afford the same states endless opportunities to discuss in various organizations various aspects of the same problem. U.S. leadership, based on a clear, attractive strategy, is often a prerequisite for action. Absent such leadership, as illustrated by civilian implementation during the first year in Bosnia, even otherwise willing states may fall into a morass of endless discussion.

It is, of course, too early to draw definitive lessons from an operation that is still unfolding. The United States might have terminated its military commitment after one year, as originally announced. In this case, other European states would almost certainly have withdrawn their forces also, and the parties would quickly have abandoned even the pretext of implementing the civilian provisions of the Dayton Agreement. Whether they would also have fought again is conjectural. Once the Eastern Slavonia question was resolved, Croatia and Serbia seemed to have little motive to fight or to support offensives by their respective peoples in Bosnia. Instead, the United States chose to assume leadership of a long-term, open-ended effort to implement the entire Dayton Agreement, centering on a common government of peoples who showed little inclination to live together. Much hangs on the success of this policy. If the United Nations, NATO, and the great powers of Europe formally united in a Peace Implementation Council, all led in various ways by the United States, cannot bring parties to embrace the values of Western civilization, then all such efforts must appear quixotic.

Thus far, Bosnia has taught these broad lessons about complex contingencies:

- Neither the UNSC nor the NAC is effective in difficult situations unless the United States leads.

- The United States cannot lead if it fails to develop a coherent strategy.

- The NSC needs strengthening to perform its statutory role in developing strategy.

- The interagency process needs strengthening: It breaks down too easily when agencies take conflicting positions or an agency carries its internal conflicts into the interagency process.

- Planning is necessary: absent a plan, departmental concerns will dominate and these may drive policy in contradictory directions.

- The United States needs a person on point with enough resources and authority to drive implementation and to represent its policy abroad.

- Ensuring good governance in a war-torn country demands years of concerted civilian-military effort.

Thus far, Bosnia has taught these lessons more explicitly directed toward civilian-military cooperation:

- Keeping military separate from civilian implementation of the same agreement is counterproductive; insulating the military from failure does not constitute success.

- Civilian-military coordination should occur at all levels, for example between State and Defense through the interagency process, high-level civilian officials and overall commanders, midlevel civilian officials and task force or sector commanders, working-level civilian officials and unit commanders.

- Given a common mission, an interagency paradigm works well in the field, i.e., equal representation on a coordinating body under the aegis of the highest-ranking official.

- Military forces cannot avoid law enforcement roles if violence threatens to become widespread.

- A bridging force is required to fill the gap between military forces and indigenous police that may be unreliable, corrupt, or repressive.

Organization of Complex Contingency Operations

There is no one right way to organize complex contingency operations. The most appropriate and effective organization will vary according to the nature of the contingency, phase of the operation, level and extent of U.S. participation, and responses from other countries. However, some general principles apply:

- If military forces have to enforce anything (e.g., agreement among parties, resolution of the Security Council, international law), they should be controlled by an appropriate agent (e.g., lead country, coalition of countries, regional security organization), not by the United Nations, which lacks the capability to conduct combat.

- Command and control arrangements should observe unity of command and be kept as simple as possible. Military forces cannot operate effectively under arrangements that require approvals from disparate agencies or lengthy deliberations.

- Transition in control, e.g., from a lead country or regional organization to the United Nations, should occur only when appropriate conditions are met, and there should be temporal overlap to smooth the transition.

- Military support to civilian implementation, especially to law enforcement, should be planned in advance and coordinated through operations centers, task forces, or other ad hoc entities.

- The civilian chief of mission (e.g., Special Representative of the U.N. Secretary General, U.S. Ambassador, uniquely established position) should have authority commensurate with his responsibility and be linked to the force commander.

It might be argued that these principles assume the outcome of a policy debate that cannot be anticipated. For example, the United States initially separated the military and civilian sides of Dayton implementation in part because U.S. officials, especially within DoD, thought the High Representative was headed for disaster and wanted to insulate the military from failure. But general principles ought to assume that the operation in both its civilian and military aspects could succeed and that the United States wants success.

Without presuming to capture the exquisite variety of complex contingency operations, a highly simplified diagram may reveal some of their characteristic features. Figure 4.12 offers such a diagram.

Relationships are characterized in an oversimplified way as being command, direction, or coordination. Command is limited to the channels from the U.S. President to the U.S. military contingent and from other heads of state to their military contingents (not shown). The President's command over the armed forces is direct and unchallenged, yet even in this capacity a President will seldom behave in a peremptory fashion. For example, he may well hesitate to give commands that would run counter to advice from the Secretary of Defense and Chairman of the Joint Chiefs of Staff. His relationships with Congress and other heads of state are formally among equals, but when playing a strong hand

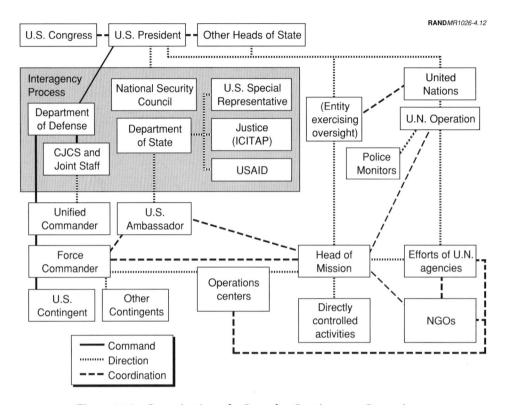

Figure 4.12—Organization of a Complex Contingency Operation

he has great influence over both. Even when there is widespread opposition to Presidential policy, Congress may hesitate to overturn it, because it has no power to pursue an alternative. Foreign heads of state, including even the French, tend to accept American lead when it seems headed for success, even if they would have preferred a different direction.

Within the interagency process, the NSC functions as the President's personal staff and should integrate departmental positions. Both civilians and military officers normally represent the Department of Defense. The Department of State plays a central role in harmonizing efforts of the civilian departments of government, and if there is a Special Representative, he will normally come from State. The State Department controls the U.S. embassy or embassies affected by the contingency and the embassy staffs include officials from other departments. In some contingencies, the U.S. ambassador might lead the effort, while in others he would coordinate with a civilian head of mission and the U.S. force commander. This civilian head might be a Special Representative of the U.N. Secretary General or he might occupy a unique position, such as the High Representative created by the Dayton Agreement. Whatever his origin, this head of mission will usually control few activities directly. For the most part, he will coordinate activities of other agencies, most importantly those of the force commander, who may be under direction (not command) of a regional alliance or, when the situation has become stable, the United Nations.

Conceptually, the head of mission, who will almost invariably be a civilian, might be supported by a combined civilian-military staff. There are disadvantages to this scheme, and it might in the end bring little improvement. First, the United States is reluctant for very good reason to accord any civilian other than the President control over U.S. forces. When, for example, U.S. forces participate in U.N.-controlled operations, as they did in Haiti, they act under orders from their own government and in doubtful cases ask for clarification through national channels. In this case, there is less real difference between formal subordination and cooperation on a basis of equality than might appear. Second, there are practical limits to civilian-military integration. Military staffs have well-defined organization and well-understood procedures to ensure that they have efficient control of forces. It would be impractical and in most cases unnecessary to integrate further than a combined operations center with suitable liaison arrangements. In the end, the most important integrative factor, indeed the indispensable foundation, is common understanding of the mission.

Chapter Five

RECOMMENDATIONS

In this chapter, we offer broad recommendations to improve coordination during complex contingency operations, especially between civilians and soldiers. These recommendations focus on development, dissemination, and implementation of U.S. policy and strategy, the indispensable foundation for any improvement.

ACHIEVE CONSENSUS ON COMPLEX CONTINGENCY OPERATIONS

The United States urgently needs national consensus, embracing Congress, opinion-makers, and the public, about the nature and scope of its role in complex contingency operations. Are they a deliberate part of U.S. foreign policy or hesitant improvisations when policy has failed? If the administration cannot obtain broad consensus, it must at least attain consensus in particular cases. Otherwise, support will remain fragile and even slight reverses may cause failure.

MAKE THE INTERAGENCY PROCESS ROBUST

The interagency process needs better definition to make it robust and productive. It should follow well-understood, firmly established procedures, not be continually reinvented in unpredictable ways. It should demand departmental advice at each level and interdepartmental decisions that are unambiguously expressed and binding on all agencies of the Executive Branch. The model offered by PDD-56 does not explicitly recognize the need for strong leadership outside the NSC structure. An optimal model would combine a Special Representative to provide leadership with a tiered system of interagency meetings to develop policy and to make day-by-day decisions.

DEVELOP AND ISSUE AUTHORITATIVE PLANS

Conduct of complex contingency operations needs formal planning to ensure that objectives are clearly understood, that actions are properly sequenced and coordinated, and that appropriate officials are held responsible for attaining objectives. PDD-56 establishes a requirement for planning but does not stipulate the authority for plans, other than the interagency process itself. As military commanders issue military plans binding on their subordinates, so the President should issue political-military plans binding on officers and officials throughout the Executive Branch. The National Security Advisor would be a natural choice for authentication of political-military plans developed through the interagency process and approved by the President.

CONDUCT ADVANCE PLANNING

PDD-56 does not specify whether planning should begin in advance or during crisis. But if planning starts during crisis, there may be insufficient time to prepare plans, coordinate the plans, and rehearse them. Therefore, the United States should plan in advance for those contingencies likely to prompt intervention. Although onset is unpredictable, it is easy to discern where complex contingencies are likely, despite early action by the United States to prevent and mitigate them. Even if future contingencies occurred in unexpected places, the discipline and experience of advance planning would be transferable to them.

BRING COMBATANT COMMANDERS INTO INTERAGENCY PLANNING

Currently, regional combatant commanders may not be directly involved in the interagency planning process or they may participate episodically. Nevertheless, these commanders have a fundamental responsibility to execute military aspects of the complex contingency operations. Moreover, they have extensive experience in their regions and routinely plan for a range of military operations, including many of the aspects associated with complex contingency operations. Working through the Joint Staff, combatant commanders and their representatives should participate directly in interagency planning.

INVITE NON-U.S. AGENCIES INTO THE PLANNING PROCESS

Non-U.S. agencies, including agencies within the United Nations system and NGOs, are usually willing to participate in a U.S.-led planning process although they are not bound by a U.S.-generated plan. For example, relief agencies are usually anxious to learn what protection will be provided and what logistic support they can expect to receive through U.S. channels. At least, relief agencies should participate during review of a political-military plan. Of course, some parts of U.S. military planning are necessarily classified, but these usually do not concern non-U.S. agencies.

ENCOURAGE CIVILIAN-MILITARY DISCOURSE

The United States needs discourse on the level of policy and strategy to achieve clarity and to bridge the civilian-military gap. Civilians should articulate goals and ask, not tell, military officers how military force can contribute to attaining them. Military officers should disabuse themselves of the notion that they need only respond to political direction: civilians badly need military advice to help develop sensible strategy.

IMPROVE INTERAGENCY TRAINING

The interagency training prescribed by PDD-56 is not funded and remains inadequately attended. It compares poorly to the more extensive training, exercises, and education conducted by military organizations. This interagency training should be appropriately funded, and participation should be mandatory or strongly encouraged. For greater realism, this training should be conducted together with a military exercise conducted by a regional combatant commander, either on-site or remotely.

ESTABLISH INTERAGENCY COMMUNICATIONS TO THE FIELD

In current practice, each department or agency of the Executive Branch has its own channel of communications to the field and there is no interagency channel, excepting communications from the President or a Special Representative speaking for him. As a result, confusion may ensue when various agencies communicate their varying interpretations of what transpired in interagency meetings. To preclude such confusion, there should be a regular channel of communications conveying decisions and instructions from interagency meetings to organizations in the field.

PROVIDE CIVILIAN SURGE CAPABILITY

During complex contingency operations, a concerned agency often forms a task force to monitor the course of events, marshal its resources, and represent the agency in the interagency process. Among the agencies of the Executive Branch, only the Department of Defense has adequate surge capability to generate such elements, especially within its military organizations that routinely generate the command and control elements of joint task forces. Other agencies lack such surge capability and therefore may not provide enough experienced personnel and adequate administrative support. There should be provision for surge capability within all agencies that expect to play important roles in complex contingency operations.

EXCHANGE PERSONNEL ACROSS DEPARTMENTS

Under current practice, the task forces or similar entities that have day-to-day responsibility for complex contingency operations may or may not include officers or officials from other agencies. It would improve communications and perhaps establish a higher level of mutual confidence, if agencies routinely loaned each other personnel. Moreover, such personnel would enrich the process by adding outside expertise. As an example, State and Defense should exchange personnel working on such task forces. In the post–Cold War era, it may also be advisable to develop a broader program of exchange across military and civilian agencies.

ENSURE COORDINATION IN THE FIELD

Coordination in the field demands that civilian heads of mission and military force commanders share strategic vision, meaning common understanding of their missions and the implied goals. In addition, they need formal arrangements to facilitate coordination, including combined operations centers, task forces, and exchange of liaison officers. These arrangements should be made in advance because the initial phase of an operation may be crucial.

CHARTER INDEPENDENT AFTER-ACTION REVIEWS

PDD-56 directs the Executive Committee to charter after-action reviews involving participants and experts, but participants should not direct or appear to direct this process. Even the military, which has an admirable tradition of after-action reporting, may occasionally portray actions as better planned, more efficiently conducted, or more successful than they were in reality, because of unit pride or command pressure. The temptation to spare people's feelings is far greater on the civilian side, where there is no comparable tradition of after-action reports. To ensure impartiality and candor, the Deputies Committee should charter consortiums of well-regarded analytic agencies to conduct reviews. These reviews will inevitably be classified, but an unclassified version should be made widely available in order to share and profit from the lessons learned.

TERMINOLOGY

This Appendix gives definitions for key terms used in the report. These are consistent with definitions contained in U.S. government White Paper, *The Clinton Administration's Policy on Managing Complex Contingency Operations*, PDD-56, The White House, May 1997, and Office of the Assistant Secretary of Defense, Strategy and Threat Reduction, Draft Working Paper, *Handbook for Interagency Management of Complex Contingency Operations*, Washington, D.C., draft dated March 1, 1998.

Table A.1

Terms and Definitions

Term	Definition
Agency plan	In the context of PDD-56, part of a political-military plan developed by a lead agency that encompasses a mission area.
Complex contingency operations	Operations to implement peace accords, e.g., Joint Endeavor Bosnia; to secure humanitarian assistance by force, e.g., Provide Comfort northern Iraq; or to assist in providing humanitarian assistance, e.g., Sea Angel in Bangladesh.
Deputies Committee	Second-highest interagency forum built around deputies of the Principals and other officers primarily at the under secretary level.
End state	In the context of PDD-56, a set of conditions that will allow the United States to terminate an operation or transfer responsibility to another entity.
Interagency process	Formal and informal rules that apply to coordination of U.S. government agencies within the Executive Branch without subordination of one agency to another.
Interagency working group	Permanent or temporary interagency body below the Deputies Committee that helps develop or implement policy, e.g., Executive Committee (ExCom), Steering Group, and Core Group.
National Security Advisor	Customary title given to the Assistant to the President for National Security Affairs, who heads the permanent staff of the National Security Council.

Table A.1—Continued

Term	Definition
National Security Council	Defined by the National Security Act of 1947 as the President, Vice President, Secretary of State, and Secretary of Defense, advised by the Chairman of the Joint Chiefs of Staff and the Director of Central Intelligence.
Political-military plan	An implementation plan to coordinate U.S. government actions in a complex contingency operation.
Principals Committee	Highest interagency forum built around statutory members of the National Security Council. All Principals may not appear, and other officers, usually at cabinet level, may be invited to appear.

OUTLINE OF A POLITICAL-MILITARY PLAN

The following outline could be used to initiate advance planning, to produce the plan required by PDD-56, or to plan in collaboration with international organizations and other states. It is based on multiple sources[1] but generally follows the scheme currently envisioned for a political-military plan.

I. INTRODUCTION

A. Character of the Contingency

Outline of a complex contingency, including its essential dynamics and how it affects or would affect U.S. interests.

B. Overview of the Plan

Authorship of the plan, outline of its structure, and statement of when the plan would be executed.

II. SITUATION ASSESSMENT

Assessment of a threatening situation, how it might evolve or has evolved into a crisis, and current U.S. policy and plans.

A. Current Situation and Trends

A comprehensive assessment of the current situation and trends that provides context for interagency planning:

---

[1] Sources include: U.S. Government White Paper, *The Clinton Administration's Policy on Managing Complex Contingency Operations*, Presidential Decision Directive–56, The White House, May 1997; National Security Council, "Generic Pol-Mil Plan," Global Issues and Multilateral Affairs, National Security Council, Washington, D.C., May 28, 1998; Office of the Assistant Secretary of Defense, Strategy and Threat Reduction, Draft Working Paper, *Handbook for Interagency Management of Complex Contingency Operations*, Washington, D.C., dated March 1, 1998; and Arthur E. ("Gene") Dewey and Walter S. Clarke, "The Comprehensive Campaign Plan: A Humanitarian/ Political/Military Partnership in 'Total Asset' Planning for Complex Humanitarian Emergencies," Congressional Hunger Center, Washington, D.C., May 1, 1997.

Political Dynamics: ideology, historical memory, alignments, and governmental structures that bear on the problem.

Military Balance: types of forces, sizes of forces, equipment holdings, training and readiness, assessment of relative combat potential, possible operations.

Economic Factors: public policy, business law, finance, international investment, imports and exports, industrial capacity, agriculture, workforce, natural resources, distribution of wealth, economic outlook.

Social and Cultural Aspects: influence of culture, tradition, historical memory, ideology, and religion; roles of social groups and institutions including family, tribes, and communities; urbanization and modernity.

Infrastructure and Environment: effects of climate and terrain, power generation and transmission, transportation systems, throughput capacity of airports and seaports, environmental issues.

Support for Peace Operations: consent of parties, consensus within the Security Council, support of regional powers and host governments, capabilities of international organizations and NGOs to support operations.

B. Crisis Scenarios

Outlines of scenarios that might prompt U.S. and international response, including outbreaks of lawlessness, collapse of existing states, armed conflict, humanitarian emergencies, large-scale violations of human rights, forced resettlement, and genocide.

C. U.S. Policy and Planning

Précis of existing policy that applies to this situation and planning already accomplished by U.S. government agencies.

III. STRATEGIC INTENT

Highest-level vision of how events will unfold to accomplish overall goals.

A. U.S. Concerns

What U.S. ideological and psychological concerns are involved (e.g., threats to democracy, violations of human rights, egregious human suffering)? How will they prompt or constrain U.S. actions?

B. U.S. Interests

What U.S. interests are at stake, how they might be affected, and what efforts would the United States exert to secure or to further them? U.S. interests may be political, e.g., leadership of an alliance; military, e.g., proliferation of weapons of mass destruction; or economic, e.g., access to markets and raw materials.

C. U.S. Strategy

How the United States envisions events unfolding to attain its purpose, including its own actions and those of others.

D. Mission

What the United States and other states intend to accomplish through complex contingency operations expressed in broad political, military, and economic terms.

E. Objectives

Measurable outcomes implied by the mission.

F. Desired End State

Conditions to terminate the operation or to transfer responsibility for continuing operations to another entity. The end state might include political settlement, stable balance of power, or economic recovery.

G. Termination or Transfer Strategy

How the United States will terminate the operation when the desired end state is attained or when it becomes unattainable. Alternatively, how the United States will transfer responsibility to another entity, such as an international organization, regional alliance, or host state.

IV. CONCEPT OF OPERATIONS

How agencies of the U.S. government, international organizations, and other states will cooperate or collaborate to accomplish the mission.

A. Phasing

Stages of the operation over time, usually defined by accomplishment of objectives within geographic areas. An illustrative set of phases appears as Table B.1.

B. Lead Agency Responsibilities

Assignment of responsibility to lead agencies in the U.S. government to accomplish tasks or to reach milestones in major functional or mission areas.

C. Organizational Concept

How agencies of the U.S. government, foreign governments, international organizations, and NGOs will be linked to conduct operations, including lines of authority and reporting channels.

Table B.1

Illustrative Phases of an Operation

Phase	Activities
I Planning	Initiate the interagency process; develop, rehearse, and review political-military plan.
II Preparation	Negotiate peace agreement, build coalition of willing countries, consult with Congress, address the American people, call up Reserve and National Guard, etc.
III Entry	Introduce forces, enforce military provisions of peace agreement, provide emergency relief, establish civilian authorities and activities, etc.
IV Restoration	Restore legitimate government, conduct electoral activities, retrain police forces, repair infrastructure, support economic recovery, etc.
V Termination	Transfer security functions, withdraw forces, establish long-term civilian and military programs to aid and advise host countries, etc.

D. Event Matrix

A matrix of events that displays time on the x-axis and actors on the y-axis. This matrix allows planners to oversee temporal relationships of interrelated events. Events include those planned for U.S. government agencies and those expected for other agencies, such as other states, international organizations, regional organizations, NGOs. An oversimplified event matrix appears as Table B.2 by way of illustration. An actual event matrix would be highly detailed, especially for initial phases of an operation.

V. PREPARATORY TASKS

Tasks that must be accomplished before operations commence, for example, negotiation of peace agreements, diplomatic consultations, coalition building, legal authority, U.S. government funding, donors' conferences, consultations with Congress, public relations, intelligence collection and analysis, etc.

VI. MISSION AREAS

Broadly defined areas within the overall mission. A lead agency writes a plan for each mission area and coordinates that plan with relevant agencies. Possible mission areas with illustrative tasks include:

A. Diplomatic Engagement (State)

Appoint a Special Representative or special envoy; lead a coalition of willing powers; arrange donors' conferences; negotiate status of forces agreements with host nations; collaborate with international organizations; mediate disagreements among former belligerents; etc.

Table B.2

Illustrative Event Matrix

Agency	Phase I (Planning)	Phase II (Preparation)	Phase III (Entry)
UNSC	Impose sanctions on belligerent parties; mediate between parties	Approve resolution authorizing Chapter VII peace operation.	Review progress of operation.
UNHCR	Help refugees secure right of asylum and find employment.	Provide continuing care to refugees who wish to return.	Promote and organize return of refugees.
World Bank	Assess needs.	Hold donors' conference.	Finance reconstruction projects.
President	Approve political-military plan.	Contact heads of state; consult with Congressional leadership; present policy to U.S. people; order selective call-up.	Visit the area of operations.
DOS	Develop portions of pol-mil plan with DOS lead; promote U.S. strategy with allies and friends.	Host peace conference; develop common policies among allies and friends; negotiate status of forces agreements.	Maintain continuing contacts with allies and friends; establish diplomatic representation with new entities.
USAID	Develop plans for humanitarian assistance and reconstruction; fund UNHCR refugee programs.	Support donors' conference; develop programs for reconstruction.	Fund reconstruction; monitor progress.
DoD	Develop and exercise military contingency plans; enforce sanctions; conduct show of force.	Establish combined and joint headquarters; receive National Guard and Reserve forces.	Deploy forces; control ports of entry and lines of communication; ensure that parties cease fire and disarm.
DOJ	Develop plan to reconstitute and reform police forces.	Train civilian police monitors; establish contacts with police.	Train and equip police; establish police academy.
DCI	Assess current situation and possible future developments.	Form interagency intelligence team; assess threats.	Produce intelligence products proactively; respond to tasking.

B. Military Security (Defense)

Show overwhelming force to former belligerents (where appropriate); provide intelligence on former belligerents; dismantle unauthorized checkpoints; confiscate illegal weapons; establish demilitarized zones; enforce cantonment of heavy weapons; disarm or demobilize forces; train and equip forces; monitor and enforce compliance with arms control agreements; maintain military-to-military contacts; assist international police monitors; patrol urban areas and lines of communication; secure evidence of war crimes; provide security to foreign officials; secure electoral activities; assist in clearing land mines; etc.

C. Weapons of Mass Destruction (Defense)

Provide intelligence on the manufacture, storage, and deployment of weapons of mass destruction (WMD); support monitors and investigators concerned with WMD; seize and secure WMD; dismantle or remove WMD; manage consequences of WMD use; etc.

D. Human Rights (State)

Monitor human rights practices; appoint Special Rapporteur or Special Prosecutor; establish a truth commission; support an international tribunal; investigate violations of human rights; apprehend suspected violators of human rights; train officials in observance of human rights, secure release of political prisoners; etc.

E. Humanitarian Assistance (USAID, OFDA)

Fund relief efforts by international organizations and NGOs; establish Civil-Military Operations Centers (CMOC) to coordinate efforts; provide potable water, foodstuffs, and shelter on an emergency basis; provide individual medical assistance; conduct disease control; restore waste disposal facilities on an emergency basis; locate missing persons and reunite families; repatriate or resettle refugees; promote mine awareness; etc.

F. Political Reconciliation (State)

Staff and fund new governmental structures; promote power sharing; provide technical and legal advice to government officials; support electoral activities; monitor conduct of elections; etc.

G. Public Services (USAID)

Provide essential equipment for government offices; provide salary supplements for government employees; rehabilitate municipal water supply; restore local health services; restore solid waste disposal systems; rehabilitate war veterans; revive educational institutions; provide family planning; etc.

H. Law and Order (Justice)

Train police monitors; monitor police activities; recruit and screen law enforcement personnel; establish training centers and police academies; provide training and reference materials; provide technical equipment and advisors; develop new criminal codes; unify and reform legal systems; upgrade and retrain judicial officials; etc.

I. Infrastructure (USAID)

Overlay and repair critical road and rail links; provide rolling stock; rebuild high-priority bridges and tunnels; repair pipelines and pumping stations; rehabilitate airports and seaports; restore municipal transit systems; restore electric power generation and transmission; restore telecommunications; clear land mines; rebuild and restore damaged housing; etc.

J. Economic Recovery (Treasury)

Initiate labor-intensive public works programs; guarantee foreign companies against political and war risks; provide balance of payments support; provide lines of credit; reform and create new banking systems; improve information flow on laws, regulations, and standards; draft new banking laws; update contract and enterprise laws; rebuild herds and breeding stock; restore production in basic industries; etc.

Albright, Madeleine, U.S. Ambassador to the United Nations, testimony before the International Security, International Organizations, and Human Rights Subcommittee, House Committee on Foreign Affairs, Washington, D.C., June 24, 1993.

Allard, Kenneth, *Somalia Operations: Lessons Learned*, Washington, D.C.: Institute for Strategic Studies, National Defense University, 1995.

Ascher, William, and William H. Overholt, *Strategic Planning and Forecasting: Political Risk and Economic Opportunity*, New York: John Wiley & Sons, 1983.

Asmus, Ronald D., *The New U.S. Strategic Debate*, Santa Monica, Calif.: RAND, MR-240-1-A, Santa Monica, CA, 1994.

Bennet, James, "Clinton to Extend U.S. Troop Mission in Bosnia," *New York Times*, December 18, 1997, p. 1.

Berger, Samuel R., "Press Briefing by National Security Advisor Sandy Berger and Special Representative to the President and Secretary of State for Implementation of the Dayton Peace Accords Robert Gelbard," Office of the Press Secretary, The White House, December 18, 1997.

Bert, Wayne, *The Reluctant Superpower: United States' Policy in Bosnia, 1991–95*, New York: St. Martin's Press, 1997.

Blank, Blanche, *It Takes Two to Tango: International Perspectives on the United Nations*, Washington, D.C.: The Fund for Peace, 1998.

Bowens, Glenn, Capt., USA, *Legal Guide to Peace Operations*, Carlisle Barracks, Pa.: U.S. Army Peacekeeping Institute, 1998.

Carnegie Commission on Preventing Deadly Conflict, *Preventing Deadly Conflict: Final Report*, New York: Carnegie Corporation of New York, 1997.

Cervenak, Christine M., *Learning on the Job: Organizational Interaction in El Salvador, 1991–1995*, Cambridge, Mass.: Conflict Management Group, 1997.

Clarke, Walter S., *Humanitarian Intervention in Somalia, Bibliography*, Carlisle Barracks, Pa.: U.S. Army War College, Center for Strategic Leadership, 1995.

Commission on America's National Interests, *America's National Interests*, Cambridge, Mass.: John F. Kennedy School of Government, Harvard University, 1996.

Corr, Edwin G., and Stephen Sloan, eds., *Low-Intensity Conflict: Old Threats in a New World*, Boulder, Colo.: Westview Press, 1992.

Crocker, Chester A., and Fen Osler Hampson, eds., *Managing Global Chaos: Sources of and Responses to International Conflict*, Washington, D.C.: United States Institute of Peace Press, 1996.

Cruger, J. King, "New Force for Bosnia Peace," *European Stars and Stripes*, August 11, 1998, p. 1.

Davis, Lois M., Susan D. Hosek, M. G. Tate, M. Perry, G. Hepler, and P. Steinberg, *Army Medical Support for Operations Other Than War*, Santa Monica, Calif.: RAND, MR-773-A, 1996.

Davis, Paul K., *New Challenges for Defense Planning: Rethinking How Much Is Enough*, Santa Monica, Calif.: RAND, MR-400-RC, 1994.

Demichelis, Julia, "NGOs and Peacebuilding in Bosnia's Ethnically Divided Cities," Washington, D.C.: United States Institute of Peace, 1998.

Destler, I. M., *Presidents, Bureaucrats, and Foreign Policy: The Politics of Organizational Reform*, Princeton, N.J.: Princeton University Press, 1972.

Dewey, Arthur E., "USG Interagency Coordination and International Architecture: The Search for Unity of Effort," briefing presented to the Chairman of the Joint Chiefs of Staff's Peace Operations Seminar, U.S. Army Peacekeeping Institute, Carlisle Barracks, Pa., June 9, 1998.

Dewey, Arthur E., and Walter S. Clarke, "The Comprehensive Campaign Plan: A Humanitarian/Political/Military Partnership in 'Total Asset' Planning for Complex Humanitarian Emergencies," Washington, D.C.: Congressional Hunger Center, May 1, 1997.

Dworken, Jonathan T., *Military Relations With Humanitarian Relief Organizations: Observations From Restore Hope*, Alexandria, Va.: Center for Naval Analyses, 1993.

Feil, Scott R., *Preventing Genocide: How the Early Use of Force Might Have Succeeded in Rwanda*, New York: Carnegie Commission on Preventing Deadly Conflict, Carnegie Corporation of New York, 1998.

Gelbard, Robert S., "Remarks of Robert Gelbard, Special Assistant to the President for Bosnia to US Institute of Peace," February 25, 1998, United States Information Service, February 26, 1998.

General Assembly of the United Nations, *Report of the International Tribunal for the Prosecution of Persons Responsible for Serious Violations of International Humanitarian Law in the Territory of the Former Yugoslavia Since 1991*, A/52/375 S/1997/729, New York, September 18, 1997.

George, Alexander L., and Jane E. Holl, *The Warning-Response Problem and Missed Opportunities in Preventive Diplomacy*, New York: Carnegie Corporation of New York, 1997.

George, Alexander W., *Presidential Decisionmaking in Foreign Policy: The Effective Use of Information and Advice*, Boulder, Colo.: Westview Press, 1980.

Goodpaster, Andrew J., *When Diplomacy Is Not Enough: Managing Multinational Military Interventions*, New York: Carnegie Corporation of New York, 1996.

Gow, James, *Triumph of the Lack of Will: International Diplomacy and the Yugoslav War*, New York: Columbia University Press, 1997.

Halperin, Morton H., *Bureaucratic Politics and Foreign Policy*, Washington, D.C.: The Brookings Institution, 1974.

Hayes, Margaret Daly, and Gary F. Wheatley, eds., *Interagency and Political-Military Dimensions of Peace Operations: Haiti—A Case Study*, Washington, D.C.: The Center for Advanced Concepts and Technology, National Defense University, 1995.

Hill, Frederick B., L. Erick Kjonnerod, and Larry M. Forster, *Report on Interagency Training for Complex Contingency Operations*, Arlington, Va.: Foreign Service Institute, 1998.

Holbrooke, Richard, *To End A War*, New York: Random House, 1998.

Inderfurth, Karl F., and Loch K. Johnson, eds., *Decisions of the Highest Order: Perspectives on the National Security Council*, Pacific Grove, Calif.: Brooks/Cole Publishing Company, 1998.

International Monetary Fund, *Bosnia and Herzegovina—Recent Economic Developments*, Washington, D.C.: IMF Staff Country Report 96/104, 1996.

Johnston, Stanley W., Jr., *Domestic Support Operations: Military Roles, Missions, and Interface with Civilian Agencies*, Carlisle Barracks, Pa.: Army War College, 1997.

Joint Chiefs of Staff, *Doctrine for Health Services Support in Joint Operations*, Joint Publication 4-02, Washington, D.C., 1995a.

_____, *Doctrine for Joint Civil Affairs,* Joint Publication 3-57, Washington, D.C., 1995b.

_____, *Doctrine for Joint Operations,* Joint Publication 3-0, Washington, D.C., 1995c.

_____, *Interagency Coordination During Joint Operations,* Joint Publication 3-08, 2 volumes, Washington, D.C., 1996.

_____, *Joint Doctrine for Military Operations Other Than War,* Joint Publication 3-07, Washington, D.C., 1995d.

Kanter, Arnold, *Vicars and Managers: Organizing for National Security,* RAND, unpublished work, 1988.

Khalilzad, Zalmay, and Ian O. Lesser, *Sources of Conflict in the 21st Century: Regional Futures and U.S. Strategy,* Santa Monica, Calif.: RAND, MR-897-AF, 1998.

Kitfield, James, "Standing Apart," *National Journal,* Vol. 30, No. 24, June 13, 1998, pp. 1350–1358.

Kugler, Richard L., *U.S. Military Strategy and Force Posture for the 21st Century: Capabilities and Requirements,* Santa Monica, Calif.: RAND, MR-328-JS, 1994.

Kumar, Krishna (team leader), *Rebuilding Postwar Rwanda: The Role of the International Community,* Washington, D.C.: A.I.D. Special Study Report No. 76, U.S. Agency for International Development, July 1996.

Kunder, James (rapporteur), *How Can Human Rights Be Better Integrated Into Peace Processes?* Washington, D.C.: The United States Institute of Peace, Washington, D.C., 1998.

Levin, Norman D., ed., *Prisms & Policy: U.S. Security Strategy After the Cold War,* Santa Monica, Calif.: RAND, MR-365-A, 1994.

Lowman, Warren, *Operations Other Than War: An Interagency Imperative,* Newport, R.I.: Naval War College, 1994.

Lute, Douglas E., *Improving National Capability to Respond to Complex Emergencies: The U.S. Experience,* New York: Carnegie Corporation of New York, 1998.

Marks, Edward, and William Lewis, *Triage for Failing States,* Washington, D.C.: National Defense University, McNair Paper 26, 1994.

McGinn, John G., "After the Explosion: International Action in the Aftermath of Nationalist War," *National Security Studies Quarterly,* Vol. 4, No. 1, Winter 1998.

McNamara, Robert S., with Brian VanDeMark, *In Retrospect: The Tragedy and Lessons of Vietnam*, New York: Random House, 1995.

Mercier, Michèle, *Crimes Without Punishment: Humanitarian Action in Former Yugoslavia*, London: Pluto Press, 1995 (initially published as *Crimes sans châtiment*, Bruylant, Brussels, and L.D.G.J., Paris: 1994).

Metz, Steven, et al., *The Future of American Landpower: Strategic Challenges for the 21st Century Army*, Carlisle Barracks, Pa.: Strategic Studies Institute, U.S. Army War College, 1996.

National Security Council, "Generic Pol-Mil Plan," paper, Office of Global Issues and Multilateral Affairs, Washington, D.C., May 28, 1998c.

_____, "Generic Pol-Mil Staff Estimate," paper, Office of Global Issues and Multilateral Affairs, Washington, D.C., draft April 10, 1998b.

_____, "PDD-25 U.S. Policy Considerations and PDD-56 Interagency Management of Complex Contingency Operations," information briefing, Office of Global Issues and Multilateral Affairs, Washington, D.C., 1998.

Natsios, Andrew S., *U.S. Foreign Policy and the Four Horsemen of the Apocalypse: Humanitarian Relief in Complex Emergencies*, Westport, Conn.: published with the Center for Strategic and International Studies by Praeger, 1997.

Oakley, Robert B., Michael J. Dziedzic, and Eliot M. Goldberg, eds., *Policing the New World Disorder: Peace Operations and Public Security*, Washington, D.C.: National Defense University Press, 1998.

Office of the Assistant Secretary of Defense, Strategy and Threat Reduction, *Handbook for Interagency Management of Complex Contingency Operations*, draft working paper, Washington, D.C., draft dated March 1, 1998.

O'Hanlon, Michael, *Saving Lives with Force: Military Criteria for Humanitarian Intervention*, Washington, D.C.: Brookings Institution Press, 1997.

Parks, Brig. Gen. Garry L., USMC, "Complex Contingency Operations, Multi-Agency Support Team," briefing prepared by The Joint Staff, (J-5, Politico-Military Affairs–Global), Washington, D.C., April 23, 1998.

Powell, Colin, with Joseph E. Persico, *My American Journey*, New York: Random House, 1995.

Sancton, Thomas, and Gilles Delafon, "The Hunt for Karadzic," *Time*, Vol. 152, No. 6, August 10, 1998, p. 68.

Seiple, Chris, *The U.S. Military/NGO Relationship in Humanitarian Interventions*, Carlisle Barracks, Pa.: U.S. Army Peacekeeping Institute, Center for Strategic Leadership, U.S. Army War College, 1996.

Seybolt, Taylor B., *Coordination in Rwanda: The Humanitarian Response to Genocide and Civil War*, Cambridge, Mass.: Conflict Management Group, 1997.

Stimson Center, "Peacekeeping and the US National Interest," report on Working Group co-chaired by Sen. Nancy L. Kassebaum and Rep. Lee H. Hamilton, The Henry L. Stimson Center, Washington, D.C., 1994.

Thornberry, Cedric, "Facilitating Cooperation in Multinational Operations," paper presented to the Chairman of the Joint Chiefs of Staff's Peace Operations Seminar, U.S. Army Peacekeeping Institute, Carlisle Barracks, Pa., June 10, 1998.

Ullman, Richard H., *The World and Yugoslavia's Wars*, New York: Council on Foreign Relations, 1996.

U.N. Security Council, *Report of the Secretary General on the United Nations Mission in Haiti*, S/1995/614, New York, July 24, 1995.

U.S. Agency for International Development, "The USAID FY 1998 Congressional Presentation," Washington, D.C., 1998.

U.S. Army, *Field Manual 100-23, Peace Operations*, Headquarters, Department of the Army, Washington, D.C., 1994.

U.S. Army Combined Arms Command, Center for Army Lessons Learned, *Operation Restore Hope*, revised final draft date August 16, 1993, Fort Leavenworth, Kan., 1993.

U.S. Army Peacekeeping Institute, Success in Peacekeeping, *United Nations Mission in Haiti: The Military Perspective*, Carlisle Barracks, Pa.: 1996.

_____, *Fourth Annual Chairman of the Joint Chiefs of Staff Peace Operations Seminar*, Carlisle Barracks, Pa.: 1998.

U.S. Army War College, *Multinational Force Command Authorities Handbook: Proceedings of the Central Region–Chiefs of Army Staff (CR-CAST) Working Group on Command Authorities Required for a Multinational Force Commander*, Carlisle Barracks, Pa.: U.S. Army War College, 1995.

U.S. Central Command, "Terms of Reference for US Forces in Somalia, United Nations Operation in Somalia Force Command," signed by Gen. J. P. Hoar, USA, Commander in Chief, Tampa, Fla., April 29, 1993.

U.S. Department of Justice, International Criminal Investigative Training Assistance Program (ICITAP), "Republic of Haiti Police Development Project," Washington, D.C., September 23, 1993.

U.S. General Accounting Office, *United Nations: U.S. Participation in Peacekeeping Operations*, Washington, D.C.: GAO/NSIAD-92-247, 1992.

_____, *U.N. Peacekeeping: Lessons Learned In Managing Recent Missions*, Washington, D.C.: GAO/NSIAD-94-9, 1994.

_____, *Humanitarian Intervention: Effectiveness of U.N. Operations in Bosnia*, Washington, D.C.: GAO/NSIAD-94-156Br, 1994.

_____, *Peace Operations: Update on the Situation in the Former Yugoslavia*, Washington, D.C.: GAO/NSIAD-95-148BR, 1995.

U.S. Government, Office of the Federal Register, National Archives and Records Administration, *The United States Government Manual 1996/1997*, Bernan Press, Lanham, Md., 1996.

U.S. Government White Paper, "The Clinton Administration's Policy on Managing Complex Contingency Operations, Presidential Decision Directive–56," The White House, May 1997.

Vance, Cyrus R., and David A. Hamburg, *Pathfinders for Peace: A Report to the UN Secretary-General on the Role of Special Representatives and Personal Envoys*, New York: Carnegie Corporation of New York, 1997.

Vick, Alan, David T. Orletsky, Abram N. Shulsky, and John Stillion, *Preparing the U.S. Air Force for Military Operations Other Than War*, Santa Monica, Calif.: RAND, MR-842-AF, 1997.

Wilson, James Q., *Bureaucracy: What Government Agencies Do and Why They Do It*, New York: HarperCollins, 1989.

World Bank, *Bosnia and Herzegovina: The Priority Reconstruction and Recovery Program: The Challenges Ahead*, Washington, D.C.: World Bank, European Commission, and the European Bank for Reconstruction and Development, 1996.

_____, *Bosnia and Herzegovina: The Priority Reconstruction Program*, Washington, D.C.: 1996.

_____, *Bosnia and Herzegovina: Implementation of the Priority Reconstruction Program in 1996, Status Report to the Donor Community*, Washington, D.C.: European Commission and the Central Europe Department of The World Bank, 1997.

_____, *Implementation of the Priority Reconstruction Program in Bosnia and Herzegovina: First Status Report to the Donor Community*, Washington, D.C.: European Commission and The World Bank in partnership with the Government of Bosnia and Herzegovina, 1996.

_____, *Bosnia and Herzegovina: The Priority Reconstruction Program: From Emergency to Sustainability*, 3 volumes, Washington, D.C.: European Commission and the Central Europe Department of The World Bank, 1997.

_____, *Bosnia and Herzegovina: From Recovery to Sustainable Growth,* Washington, D.C.: 1997.